Keynes on the Wireless

Keynes on the Wireless

John Maynard Keynes

Edited by

Donald Moggridge

palgrave
macmillan

First published 2010 by
PALGRAVE MACMILLAN

Palgrave Macmillan in the UK is an imprint of Macmillan Publishers Limited,
registered in England, company number 785998, of Houndmills, Basingstoke,
Hampshire RG21 6XS.

Palgrave Macmillan in the US is a division of St Martin's Press LLC,
175 Fifth Avenue, New York, NY 10010.

Palgrave Macmillan is the global academic imprint of the above companies
and has companies and representatives throughout the world.

Palgrave® and Macmillan® are registered trademarks in the United States,
the United Kingdom, Europe and other countries.

ISBN: 978–0–230–23916–6 hardback

This book is printed on paper suitable for recycling and made from fully
managed and sustained forest sources. Logging, pulping and manufacturing
processes are expected to conform to the environmental regulations of the
country of origin.

A catalogue record for this book is available from the British Library.

A catalog record for this book is available from the Library of Congress.

10 9 8 7 6 5 4 3 2 1
19 18 17 16 15 14 13 12 11 10

Printed and bound in Great Britain by
CPI Antony Rowe, Chippenham and Eastbourne

Contents

Introduction[1]

Donald Moggridge

Maynard Keynes's most active years as a public intellectual coincided with the rise of a new medium – the wireless, as it was called in Britain. Between January 1925 and July 1945 he made 21 broadcasts.[2] All but one of these were for the British

---

[1] In the notes which follow, all references to material in this volume will take the form of the page number; references to *The Collected Writings of John Maynard Keynes* (eds. Elizabeth Johnson and Donald Moggridge), London: Macmillan, 1971–89 will take the form of a roman numeral for the volume number followed by the page number; references to the Keynes Papers in the Modern Archive Centre at King's College, Cambridge will take the form KCKP followed by the file number and the document(s) concerned. Unpublished writings by J.M. Keynes copyright the Provost and Scholars of King's College, Cambridge, 2010.

[2] He was also the subject of two movie interviews: one in March 1930 discussing reparations with some King's undergraduate economists, which has not survived, and one at the end of September 1931, discussing Britain's departure from the gold standard. There is a clip of the September 1931 Movitone in the DVD *John Maynard Keynes: Life – Ideas – Legacy*, written and introduced by Mark Blaug, London: Institute of Economic Affairs, 1988. A portion of the broadcast 'The Arts Council: Its

Broadcasting Corporation or its predecessor the British Broadcasting Company.

Initially, Keynes was not the ideal potential commentator on current affairs, for both the Company's and then the Corporation's freedom to broadcast were strictly limited. Under the terms of the Corporation's initial licence, it had to abstain from 'statements expressing the opinion of the Corporation on matters of public policy' and from 'speeches or lectures containing statements on topics of political, religious or industrial controversy'.[3] Only on 5 March 1928 did the Prime Minister announce that while the BBC would continue to be prohibited from expressing any view on public policy, the ban on broadcasting controversial matters was being removed 'experimentally' on the understanding that the BBC would use the discretionary power entrusted to it responsibly.[4]

Keynes's first broadcast on 'Inter-Allied Debts' on 9 January 1925 ran into 'controversy' problems, for it took place during Anglo-French negotiations in Paris on France's war debt to England. He was warned by his former Treasury colleague S.D. Waley that 'your utterances will not be welcome in the highest

Policy and Hopes' in the British Library's The Spoken Word series on *The Bloomsbury Group*. CD 1.
[3] Asa Briggs, *The History of Broadcasting in the United Kingdom, Volume II, The Golden Age of the Wireless*, London: Oxford University Press, 1965, 128.
[4] 214 HC Deb 5 s, Column 812; Michael Carney, *Stoker: The Life of Hilda Matheson OBE*, Pencaedu Llangynage: Michael Carney, 1999, 34.

quarters' and told by Edward Marsh, who had accompanied Churchill into the Treasury when he became Chancellor, that 'boss and advisers do not agree with your line and hope you will not publish suggestion at present'. His text was 'censored at the last moment by the Foreign Office on the ground that my sentiments were pro-French'. It certainly would be, as he later told Charles Siepmann of the Adult Education Section, who was trying to get him to speak again, 'tiresome to waste my time in the same way again'.[5] He was reassured that such difficulties were unlikely this time, particularly given the Prime Minister's statement of 5 March, and his May 1928 broadcast on 'The War Debts' went ahead without incident.[6] However, there were still occasional ructions, as in the fall of 1932 when his manuscript on 'The Pros and Cons of Tariffs' ran foul of the BBC's caution and an apprehensive Charles Siepmann, by then Director of Talks.

> I think we must omit the reference to Ottawa in an impartial survey of the tariff position. It is too personal and partisan a view of what is, at the moment, a matter of political controversy.[7]

---

[5] KCKP, BR/1, S.D. Waley to JMK, 7 January 1925; Edward Marsh to JMK, January 1925; JMK to C. Siepmann, 25 February 1928.
[6] KCKP, BR/1, C. Siepmann to JMK, 1 March 1928; JMK to C. Siepmann, 6 March 1928.
[7] The reference is to the 1932 Ottawa Agreements on Imperial Preference. KCKP, BR/2, C. Siepmann to JMK, 25 November 1932.

Yet on other occasions, officialdom could be helpful: in preparing his 'The World Economic Conference: A Conversation with Walter Lippmann' he consulted with Sir Frederick Leith-Ross, the Chief Economic Adviser to the Government, as 'obviously on an occasion of this sort one does not want to run counter to what is practicable. So I should like, if I could, to have a talk with you.'[8] After seeing Leith-Ross he went on to see the Prime Minister.[9]

Keynes faced other difficulties with broadcasting. His earnings from journalism formed an important part of his income in the years up to the mid-1930s when he declared he 'had now given up writing for a living, as I used to formerly' (XXVIII, 80). This meant that he was very conscious of copyright and his income from syndication. At first, despite the vagueness of the copyright protection for broadcasts, Keynes explicitly retained his rights and handled his own syndication. The BBC's initiation of its own weekly journal, *The Listener*, in January 1929 did not complicate matters domestically, for as Keynes put it[10]:

> [As] the Listener has no effective copyright of the talks in this country, my assignment to them of the first British serial rights... [is] in the nature of a bluff and not being worth very much, since

---

[8] KCKP, BR/2, JMK to Sir Frederick Leith-Ross, 18 May 1933.
[9] KCKP, BR/2, C. Siepmann to JMK, 15 May 1933.
[10] KCKP, BR/2, JMK to C. Siepmann, 21 January 1931.

there is nothing to prevent anyone in this country from taking the talks down by shorthand and publishing them anywhere.

But there was still the question of foreign rights. This had not mattered with his brief 1929 comment on Bank rate or his February 1930 discussion on unemployment with Josiah Stamp, but it became urgent in the winter of 1931, when the *New York Times* asked Keynes for a copy of the manuscript for 'Saving and Spending' which it proposed to cable to the United States. Keynes thought that the *New York Times* believed it could get the article for nothing.[11] In the end he replied that the copy would cost £25. The *New York Times* declined.[12] The issue arose again with a non-broadcast piece, 'Proposals for a Revenue Tariff' published in the *New Statesman* on 7 March. C.A. Selden of *New York Times*, at the suggestion of Kingsley Martin the editor of the *New Statesman*, asked Keynes if he could cable not more than 250 words of the article to New York. Keynes accused Selden of 'trying to interfere with ... [his] American copyright and get something for nothing'.[13] Again Seldin did not send anything even though an extract from the article had appeared in *The Times* of London with no copyright reservation and the *New York Times* had a special agreement with its

---

[11] KCKP, BR/2, JMK to Hilda Matheson, 8 and 10 January 1931.
[12] KCKP, BR/2, C.A. Selden to JMK, 13 March 1931.
[13] *Ibid.*

London namesake giving it full use of anything that appeared in the paper.

After these incidents, one solution Keynes temporarily adopted for broadcasts was to forbid publication in *The Listener*. This meant that his broadcast on 'State Planning' on 14 March 1932 did not appear there – or anywhere else. He then agreed to allow the BBC to report his talks in a shortened form in the third person 'as is commonly done by the daily press in the case of outstanding broadcast talks', but it never seems to have used this procedure.[14] On the occasion of the next broadcast, 'The Pros and Cons of Tariffs', the BBC raised Keynes's fee to 25 guineas as the price of publication in *The Listener*.[15] With the exception of the 1934 broadcast, 'Is the Economic System Self-Adjusting?', which appeared in the *New Republic* and the *Bulletin of the Antwerp Chamber of Commerce*, none of Keynes's broadcasts after the arrival of *The Listener* was published elsewhere.

In the case of 'The World Economic Conference: A Conversation with Walter Lippmann', Keynes completely wrong-footed the BBC when he proposed to waive his copyright if the BBC would make it readily available to others.[16] But Keynes continued to raise his underlying concern.[17]

---

[14] KCKP, BR/2, R.S. Lambert to JMK, 17 March and 4 April 1932, JMK to R.S. Lambert, 5 and 8 April 1932.
[15] KCKP, BR/2, J.M. Rose-Troup to JMK, 15 November 1932.
[16] KCKP, BR/2, JMK to C. Siepmann, 11 May 1933, J.M. Rose-Troup to JMK, 22 May 1933.
[17] KCKP, BR/2, JMK to J.M. Rose-Troup, 24 May 1933.

It seems to me to be necessary in dealing with professional writers to make a distinction between asking them to broadcast, which is somewhat in the nature of a public speech, and asking them to assign to you copyright at a fraction of their normal market value. I am of the opinion that the two transactions should be separated and each dealt with on its merits.[18]

Keynes's correspondence on these broadcasts often touched on another related aspect of this issue, which was also a subject of contention within the BBC – the relation between the spoken and the written word. Both Hilda Matheson and Charles Siepmann as successive Directors of Talks were 'at pains to treat the Talk as an art form; they did not care whether it read well or not, if it sounded right.' This view left an undercurrent of controversy between them and R.S. Lambert, the first editor of *The Listener*.[19] In his case, Keynes stressed the difference as a part of his argument against publishing talks.[20]

I consider it very hampering in preparing a broadcast talk to have to think of it at the same time as being an article. Except in the case of those who

---

[18] There was one final discussion of fees with the BBC, but this was for an article in a series published in *The Listener* but never broadcast – 'Art and the State' (XXVIII, 341–9). In that case, Keynes met his match in J.R. Ackerly, the Literary Editor, and lost the argument (XVIII, 335–41).

[19] Briggs, *The Golden Age of the Wireless*, 291.

[20] KCKP, BR/2, JMK to R.S. Lambert, 6 April 1932.

give talks regularly, most of which are not reprinted in 'The Listener', my feeling is that most of them write articles which they then read out loud. Any professional author given the task of preparing an address which is going to be printed immediately afterwards and have a wide circulation, is almost bound to be influenced to compose it in [an] artificial form. At any rate, I know that I have that strongly myself in the case of anything which is to be printed verbatim. This has the effect, I surmise, of greatly damaging the talks as talks. Thus I try to protect myself from the particular kind of literary influences which I know by experience will assail me if my words are to be reproduced as an article.

Except on the one occasion noted above, Keynes did not hold out against publication once *The Listener* came on the scene. However, with 'Is the Economic System Self-adjusting', which was a part of a series 'Poverty in Plenty', although he allowed publication in *The Listener*, he refused to grant publication in book form on the grounds that 'the informal talk and the written book are totally different mediums for expressing one's ideas and should not be confused and identified' and that the prospect of subsequent publication 'is likely to work to the disadvantage of the spoken word' (XIII, 485).[21]

---

[21] He provided a statement for the Editor's Foreword:
   It is simply on a point of principle, that in my opinion broadcast talks should not be made into books and that the

The broadcasts printed below are divided into five sections: War Debts, The Depression, Measures for Recovery, Education Books and the Arts, and World War II. For each section or item, where appropriate, there is an introductory note.[22] For each item we provide date of delivery and in a footnote the first British publication and its location in the *Collected Writings*. Further publication details may be found in volume XXX of that edition.

---

expectation of subsequent publication has a tendency to spoil the talk as a talk.

Graham Hutton (ed.), *The Burden of Plenty*, London: Allen & Unwin, 1935, 9.

[22] The inspiration for this volume was *John Maynard Keynes on Air: Der Weltökonom am Mikrofon der BBC* (Hamburg: Murman Verlag GmbH, 2008), which contained all the essays printed below except for 'The Inter-Allied Debts' (Part I) and 'Bretton Woods' (Part V).

I
War Debts

Keynes had made his public reputation through his resignation from the Treasury over the Treaty of Versailles in June 1919 and through his publication of *The Economic Consequences of the Peace* the following December. Thereafter he was a prolific contributor to public discussions of the post-war settlement and its subsequent revisions. However, in part because the BBC was not broadcasting anything until late 1922, he made few broadcasts on the issue.

The Inter-Allied Debts

[9 January 1925][1]

His first publication came in January 1925, By then
the reparations problem had been 'temporarily' settled by the Dawes Plan and the subsequent Dawes
Loan to Germany. Afterwards, the American Debt
Funding Commission approached France for a settlement of her war debts to the United States. France
was rumoured to be seeking more favourable terms
from the Americans than Britain had received in
1923 and the British worried about the implications
of such an agreement for France's war debts to Britain
which had still to be settled. Keynes, who had
opposed the Anglo-American agreement of January
1923, commented.

Most of the politicians and business men of America – but not all of them – tell us that they look on

---

[1] *The Nation and Athenaeum*, 10 January 1925, 516–17; XVIII,
264–8.

these debts just like any ordinary commercial debt for goods sold and delivered. We, in Great Britain, are acting on that principle. The United States have asked us to pay and we are paying. Nevertheless, there are three sufficient reasons for not treating France and Italy in a like manner – the origin of the debts, the evils which would follow on an attempt to exact them, and the practical impossibilities of collection. I sympathize, therefore, with the distinction, which M. Clémentel, the French minister of finance, has recently made, in calling these debts 'political' debts, and the other obligations of the French government 'commercial debts'. The inter-allied debts are a matter of politics and not of law or contract. It is as mistaken to treat them as things of contract as it was to treat the theoretical liabilities of Germany under the Treaty of Versailles as things of contract.

If we consider for one minute the origin of the debts, it is obvious that they are not just like other debts. Let me put the argument as it may reasonably appear to a Frenchman. Each of the Allies threw the whole of their strength into the struggle – it was, as the Americans say, a 100 per cent war. But – wisely and properly – they did not all use their strength in the same way. For example, the effort of France was mainly military. On account of the number of men she put into the field in proportion to her population, and because part of France was occupied by the enemy, France did not possess, after the first year, sufficient economic strength to equip her armies and feed her people, as well as to fight. Our military effort, though very great, was not so great as that of France; but our naval effort was much greater than hers; and our financial effort also was far greater, since it fell on us – until America came into the war – to use our wealth and our industrial strength to help to equip and feed the other Allies. America's effort, on the other hand, was mainly financial. Both absolutely and in proportion to her population, her military effort, measured by the number of men she placed in the field and by her casualties – important though it was to the result – was on an altogether smaller scale. On the other hand, the part which America played in equipping and feeding the Allies was enormous, and we could not, without such help, have won the war. Thus each Ally made essential contributions to the result. But they did not all make them in the same way.

Now it has never occurred to us or to America to charge France and Italy for the British or American shells fired off from British or American guns. Yet, when British or American shells were fired off from French or Italian guns, the real cost to us or to America was much less, since France and Italy supplied the gunners, suffered the casualties, and are paying the pensions. Yet in this case we propose to charge France and Italy for the shells. In fact, when American men and guns and shells had time to reach the front, so that France was wholly relieved within the sector which they took over, it did not even occur to anyone that France should be charged money for the aid which America thus gave to her. When Great Britain sent men as well as supplies to the Italian-front, there is no idea of charging Italy anything. But when the American men and guns had not reached the front, and only American shells or American wheat or American petrol reached the French armies, so that France had to find the men to use the equipment and to suffer the human losses, then France is to pay for the shells, the wheat, and the petrol. There is no rhyme or reason in this, no justice or common sense.

Why, then, were these sums lent, instead of being given outright at the beginning, which would have saved all this trouble? There was, at the time, an excellent reason against this – if the money had been given outright, it would certainly have promoted extravagance and a lack of responsibility in spending. A large part of the financial conduct of the war consisted in establishing financial controls, that is, in preventing one department or one Ally spending sums out of the limited total resources available, which could be spent to better advantage by another department or Ally. It was hard enough for the Treasury to control our own spending departments, and it was impossible, except indirectly, to control the spending departments of our Allies. If every official of the Allied governments, down to those with the least feeling of responsibility and the least power of imagination, had known that it was someone else's money he was spending, the incentives to economy would have been even less than they were.

I have had no connection with the British Treasury for several years. But I am sure that their dealings with their Allies during the war were mainly directed to the enforcement of necessary economy and to seeing that our limited resources were spent to the best advantage. These transactions were not looked on at the time in the light of investments or commercial advances. And, I am sure, the same was true of the American Treasury. If the American public now think that in 1917 and 1918 they were engaged, not in war, but in investment, their memories are very short.

But, apart from the history of the debts, the attempt to exact them now will have no other result than to breed international ill-will. We should just have the German reparation problem over again between each of the former Allies. Hatred, dissension, and – in my belief – not even money would be the result of trying to collect this sum year by year for a generation.

Not even money – for France not only believes conscientiously that justice does not require her to pay, and also that she cannot pay but also that payment in full would, in view of the history of German reparations, so deeply outrage her most genuine feelings that she would not do it, even if it were in her interest.

For let us look at the demand in relation to the Dawes scheme. If France were to pay interest and sinking fund, even at a low rate of interest, on what she owes to us and to the United States, it would come to rather more than £60 million a year, which is almost exactly equal to the *whole* of France's share of German reparations under the Dawes scheme, on the assumption that this scheme works out in full. Does anyone believe that France, in whatever circumstances or under whatever threats, will agree to hand over to Great Britain and the United States every penny that she gets from Germany, and perhaps more?

What, then, ought we to do? Looking back, I believe that it would have been an act of statesmanship and wisdom on the part of Great Britain if, on the day of the Armistice, we had announced to our Allies that all they owed us was forgiven from that day. It is not easy to take that line now. For one thing, we ourselves have undertaken to pay to America half a million dollars every weekday for sixty years, and day by day we are paying it. This sum is equivalent to two-thirds of the cost of our navy and is nearly equal to the total of our State expenditure on education. It is more than the whole of the profits of all our merchant ships and all our coal mines added together. With an equal sacrifice over an equal period we could abolish slums and rehouse our population in comfort. That we should pay on this scale, and not be paid ourselves, must influence our attitude. Therefore, the idea that America should get better terms from France than we gét, because of her brusquer attitude, is, for good reasons, intolerable to British opinion. It is impossible, now, for us to forgive the debts of France and of

Italy unless America does the same. We cannot tolerate even the suggestion that America, whom we are paying, should get better terms than we get from those who owe us both. A frank discussion between Great Britain and America must, therefore, be the first step to a settlement. And if I may make a suggestion as to the lines of compromise which such a settlement might take, it is this: let a certain moderate proportion of what France and Italy may receive from Germany each year, out of payments made under the Dawes scheme, be devoted to the payment of the French and Italian debts to their Allies; let these sums be divided between Great Britain and the United States in the proportion of what each is owed; and let this be in final discharge.

It is not appropriate to invite France to make an offer, as the American Debt Funding Commission is now doing. For this is merely to ask France to expose herself to humiliation. But if Great Britain and the United States could agree together to make to her a proposal on the above lines – say, one-third of what she may receive from Germany from time to time hereafter – there is a chance of an honourable settlement.

The War Debts

[3 May 1928][1]

By the time Keynes returned to the subject on air, it was clear that the 'temporary' Dawes settlement would soon be up for revision. Not only was it necessary to set a final figure for German reparations payments but also a need to end the Dawes Plan's provisions for the international supervision of the Reichsbank and the German railways and the earmarking of particular taxes to meet reparation payments in perpetuity. There was also growing apprehension that Germany would not be able to keep borrowing abroad to meet its reparations payments as well as its current account deficit on the balance of payments as it had been doing since 1925, which, given the transfer protection provisions of the Dawes Plan that allowed the Agent-General for Reparations to postpone reparation payments raised in Germany into foreign currency if this would threaten the exchange rate. This left the level of

[1] *The Nation and Athenaeum*, 5 May 1928, 131–3; IX, 47–53.

reparations payments available to recipients in any year to pay their war debts to Britain and the United States uncertain. At the same time German public opinion also demanded a reduction in its reparations payments from the levels set out in the Dawes Plan, which as Keynes pointed out (27) might affect their ability to meet payments on their war debts.

Keynes's talk was the first of six on 'Modern Aspects of Finance'.

For the moment there is a lull in the acrid discussion which, now for nine years, has been waged around this question. But it has not been put to rest for long, and the time for its revival will undoubtedly come when the Dawes Scheme is up for revision – as sooner or later, and sooner better than later, it must be. It is opportune, therefore, to take stock of the situation as the negotiations of several years have left it.

Let us remember the origin of these debts. Soon after the beginning of the war it was clear that certain of our Allies – Russia and Belgium in the first instance, but subsequently all of them – would require financial assistance. We might have given this in loans or in subsidies. Loans were preferred to subsidies, in order to preserve a greater sense of responsibility and economy in the spending of them. But though financial assistance took the form of loans, it is scarcely to be supposed that the lending countries regarded them at the time as being in the nature of ordinary investments. Indeed, it would have been very illogical to do so. For we often gave assistance in the form of money, precisely because we were less able to assist with men or ships. For example, when we sent guns to Italy to help her after her first serious reverse, she had to pay for them by loans. But when matters got worse still, and we sent not only guns but also gunners to man them and to be killed, we charged nothing. Yet in the former case Italy's contribution was the greater and in the latter ours. In particular, America's contribution for some time after she came into the war was mainly financial, because she was not yet ready to help in any other way. So long as America was sending materials and munitions to be used by Allied soldiers, she charged us for them, and these charges are the origin of what we now owe her. But when later on she sent men too, to use the munitions themselves, we were charged nothing. Evidently there is not much logic in a system which causes us to owe money to America, not because she was able to help us so much, but because at first she was able to help us, so far at least as manpower was concerned, so little.

This does not mean that the financial help which America gave us was not of the most extraordinary value to us. By the time America came into the war our own resources as a lender were literally at an end. We were still just about able to finance ourselves, but we had reached a point before we could no longer finance our Allies. America's financial assistance was therefore quite invaluable. From the moment she entered the war she undertook to lend on whatever was required for ourselves and our Allies in the United States, including some contribution to support the foreign exchanges. However, she was not prepared to make loans for use outside America. Great Britain had, therefore, to go on making loans to her Allies for such expenditure – with the result that we had to lend our Allies, after America came into the war, an amount almost equal to what we ourselves borrowed. More precisely, we borrowed from the United States, after she came into the war, £850 million, and lent £750 million to our Allies during the same period; so that in effect it was true – what the Americans have always been concerned to deny – that the loans she made to us were for the purpose of financing our Allies rather than for ourselves.

The result was that by the end of the war we were owed by our Allies about £1,600 million, while we, in our turn, owed to the United States only £850 million.

Since the war, the question has been constantly debated over whether these sums ought to be treated as investments, just like any other business transaction, or whether regard should be paid to their origin and to the circumstances in which they were made. It has been the British view that they were not made as business transactions and therefore should not be treated so. It has been the American view, on the other hand, that they should be taken at their face value, that is to say, as bonds due and payable, tempered only by considerations as to the capacity of the debtor to pay and, in practice, by a willingness on the part of the United States to accept a low rate of interest.

During the Peace Conference, the British government urged that the Allied war debts should be entirely cancelled. Mr Lloyd George raised the matter again with President Wilson in August 1920. Finally, in August 1922, in the famous Note written by Lord Balfour, the considered British view, from which we have never gone back, was set forth. In this Note the British government declared their willingness to cancel the whole of what their allies owed them, and also to forgo their own claims on Germany in favour of the other Allies, if the United States in turn would relieve them of their debt. By such an arrangement Great Britain would have been giving up on paper more than twice what she gained. The offer still holds good.

This policy was not accepted by the United States, and a separate settlement has been made between each pair of countries in turn. The settlement made with Great Britain is equivalent to charging a rate of interest of 3·3 per cent on the whole amount due. The American settlement with France is equivalent to repayment at 1·6 per cent interest, and that with Italy to repayment at 0·4 per cent interest. Thus, the American settlement with Great Britain is twice as onerous as that with France and eight times as onerous as that with Italy. Great Britain, in her turn, has made arrangements with France and Italy, and has in both cases let them off lighter even than has the

United States – the British settlement with France being 10 per cent easier and that with Italy 33 per cent easier than the corresponding American settlements. Thus, while the other Allies have been largely relieved, this country is left with the task of repaying her whole burden, subject only to the mitigation that the rate of interest charged, namely, 3·3 per cent, is moderate.

The effect of this settlement is that Great Britain will have to pay to the United States a sum of about £33 million annually up to 1933, rising to nearly £38 million annually thereafter from that year until 1984, when the debt will have been discharged. The reality of the weight of this burden may be illustrated by certain calculations which I made in the summer of 1923 when the details of Mr Baldwin's settlement with Washington were first made public. We shall be paying to the United States each year for sixty years a sum equivalent to two-thirds of the cost of our Navy, a sum nearly equal to our State expenditure on education, a sum which exceeds the total burden of our pre-war debt. Looked at from another standpoint, it represents more than the total normal profits of our coal mines and our mercantile marine added together. With these sums we could endow and splendidly house *every month* for sixty years one new university, one new hospital, one new institute of research, etc. etc. With an equal sacrifice, over an equal period we could abolish slums and re-house in comfort the half of our population which is now inadequately sheltered.

On the other hand, we are now receiving from our Allies and from Germany an important contribution as an offset to what we ourselves pay to the United States. It will be interesting to establish a rough balance sheet.

In 1928 we shall receive from our Allies £12,800,000 and pay the United States £33,200,000; and by 1933 these figures will have risen to £17,700,000 and £37,800,000. Thus apart from our share of German reparations, we shall be paying annually in respect of war debts about £20 million more than we receive. Now if the Dawes annuities are paid by Germany in full, we shall come out just about 'all-square'. For the normal Dawes annuity when it has reached its full figure (less the service of German loans, etc.) will amount to £117 million, of which our share (excluding the receipts of other parts of the Empire) will be about £22 million. Mr Churchill has estimated that in the current financial year, 1928–9, our payments out will be £32,845,000, and our total receipts nearly £32 million.

It is not probable that these receipts will be realised in full. But it will enable us to summarise the situation if we assume for the moment that they are so realised. In this case, each Ally would be able to pay the United States out of their receipts from Germany. When the Allied debt payments to the United States have reached their maximum amount under the existing settlements, they will total to £83 million per annum (the *average* amount payable annually over the whole period works out at a total of £61 million). If we add to this the direct American share in German reparations, the United States will be receiving £78 million annually out of the £117 million receivable by the Allies from Germany, or 67 per cent, *plus* £10 million from Italy not covered by reparations; or if we take the average payments, in lieu of the maximum, the United States will be receiving £66 million out of £117 million or 57 per cent. In either case Great Britain would receive, on balance, nothing.

It follows from the above that if the maximum Dawes annuities were to be reduced by one-third – which, in the opinion of many of us, is highly prob-able – the United States will, by the time that the Allied payments to her have reached their full fig-ure, be the sole beneficiary. In this event the net result of all war debt settlements would be to leave the United States – on balance and off-setting receipts against payments – receiving from Germany £78 million per annum, and no one else getting any-thing.

I have put the calculation in this form because it renders it very clear why, in the minds of the Allies, the question of further relief to Germany is inti-mately bound up with the question of their own obligations to the United States. The official American attitude that there is no connection between the two, is a very hollow pretence. The resettlement of the Dawes Scheme is one to which the United States must be, in one way or another, a party. But – let me add – any concession she may make will go entirely to the relief of Germany and the European Allies, Great Britain adhering to her principle of receiving nothing on balance.

If all, or nearly all, of what Germany pays for reparations has to be used, not to repair the damage done, but to repay the United States for the financial part which she played in the common struggle, many will feel that this is not an outcome tolerable to the sentiments of mankind or in reasonable accord with the spoken professions of Americans when they entered the war or afterwards. Yet it is a delicate matter, however keenly the public may feel, for any Englishman in authority to take the initiative in saying such things in an official way. Obviously, we must pay what we have covenanted to pay, and any proposal, if there is to be one, must come from the United States. It fell to my lot during the war to be the official draftsman in the British Treasury of all the financial agreements with the Allies and with the United States out of which this situation has arisen. I was intimately familiar, day by day, with the reasons and motives which governed the character of the financial arrangements which were made. In the light of the memories of those days, I continue to hope that in due course, and in her own time, America will tell us that she has not spoken her last word.

In fact a new committee of experts under Owen D. Young was appointed in September 1928 and met for the first time in Paris on 9 February 1929. The resulting Young Plan came into operation in May 1930. The Lausanne Conference saw the effective end of reparations in July 1932, although Germany did not complete her repayment of the international loans Germany received under the Dawes and Young Plans until 1 June 1980.

II
The Depression

The Bank Rate

[27 September 1929][1]

During the latter part of 1928 and 1929, the Wall Street boom and the collapse of American foreign lending put great pressure on the British balance of payments and led to a substantial fall in Britain's international reserves. Bank rate, which had been set at 4½ per cent on 21 April 1927, went up to 5½ per cent on 7 February 1929 and, after a great struggle to avoid it, to 6½ per cent, its highest level since 1921, on 26 September.

I have been set a difficult – perhaps an impossible – task in being expected to say something simple and intelligible about the consequences of the increase of Bank rate from 5½ per cent to 6½ per cent, which is announced in this morning's papers. For the theory of Bank rate is not like – shall we say? – astronomy, a matter where there is an

---

[1] *The Listener*, 2 October 1929, 435; XIX, 834–8.

ascertained true doctrine with which all experts agree. It is at present, unfortunately, much more like theology. For it is not only obscure – but also extremely controversial. Yet I do not want this evening to bring in controversy where I can avoid it. It is my duty to try to explain to you some of the consequences of Bank rate without praising or blaming them.

Bank rate has been raised because gold has been flowing out of the Bank of England on a large scale to meet payments due to foreign countries. The Bank has lost more than £40,000,000 in a year, which is nearly a quarter of its total stock. Why has gold been flowing out? Because we owe foreign countries more than they owe us. But why on balance are we debtors to foreign countries?

On trading account foreign countries are usually debtors to us. For the sums we earn as interest on our foreign investment – for our services to the world as shipowners and business men and in payment for our exports – are greater than what we spend on our imports and our tourist expenditure and so forth – greater by between £100,000,000 and £150,000,000 a year. This means that we are in a position to lend to foreign countries on capital account an amount equal to this favourable surplus of our trading account. If we lend more than this, *we* must pay *them* the difference in gold.

Since there are innumerable transactions both ways, it is practically impossible to get any direct knowledge how much we are lending on balance. But if gold is flowing out and continues to flow out on a large scale, as it has in recent months, this proves that we are lending on capital account more than our surplus on trading account.

If this is due to temporary causes, we can afford to let the gold go for a time – that is the purpose for which we hold gold reserves; or the Bank of England could borrow abroad to balance the temporary deficiency. But if the trouble is thought to be too deep-seated for these expedients to be suitable, then there are only two remedies: either we must lend less on capital account, or we must have a larger surplus in our favour on trading account. Now, how much we lend on capital account depends on whether our terms for lending are cheap compared with those abroad. And how large our surplus is on trading account chiefly depends on whether our costs of production of the goods which enter into international trade are low compared with those abroad. That is to say – in order to right the balance – we must either lend our money dearer or sell our goods cheaper.

Now, the importance of Bank rate is that it affects the rate at which the banks lend money. The immediate reason, therefore, why it is a remedy for a loss of gold is because, by raising the terms on which we lend money to foreigners, it causes them to borrow less from us. But there is also a secondary and much more complicated reason why Bank rate is a remedy, namely, that if it is carried to its logical conclusion, it may cause us in the long run to sell more cheaply and so to increase the favourable balance on trading account which is the source of our ability to lend abroad.

That the immediate and direct effect of Bank rate is to cause us to lend less abroad there is, and can be, no doubt. The difficult thing to understand and explain is its indirect effect. How can it be that Bank rate tends to reduce our costs of production, when it starts off by doing the exact opposite – for it increases one of the costs of production, namely, the cost of interest? This is what I must try to explain. For it is entirely in the indirect effects that the troublesome consequences of Bank rate are to be found.

We have seen that when the Bank rate is raised, it costs more to borrow money, and this deters foreign borrowers. But it also deters home borrowers – particularly if the cost is raised to a figure so high that it has only been equalled in the past for short periods and in times of grave crisis – which is true of the present 6½ per cent rate. If home borrowers are discouraged by the high rate, then fewer orders are placed, new projects are put off and consequently employment is decreased. But how does this help us to attain our goal of reducing our costs of production? This only comes about if unemployment rises to so high a figure and continues for so long a time that wages are forced down. Then, indeed, our costs of production are decreased, so that we are able to sell more abroad. Thus the effect of a high Bank rate is to discourage borrowing and to cause the postponement of new enterprises. So far as this affects borrowing by foreigners, it removes the strain on the Bank of England's gold. But in so far as it affects borrowing at home, it causes business losses and increases unemployment.

Left to itself the Bank rate inevitably produces both sets of consequences. The first thing, therefore, which our authorities have to decide is whether they desire both sets or only the first. Some people think that our wages are too high and ought to be reduced. If so, then both sets of consequences are desired, for it is difficult to see how wages can be reduced except by the pressure of increasing unemployment. In this case we must not complain if unemployment increases, for this is part of the mighty process, part of the process of restoring international equilibrium by reducing British wages. But if we decide that we desire only the first set, namely, the reduction of foreign lending, then we must accompany the increase of Bank rate with other measures intended to counteract so far as possible its effect on enterprise at home.

I think it is true to say that the intention of the authorities today is to produce the first set of consequences, namely, the reduction of foreign lending, and not the second set, namely, the reduction of enterprise and employment at home. The question is: How far is it practicable for them to do the one and not the other?

In so far as the Bank of England can increase the rate of interest without restricting the volume of credit – so that all home borrowers who are ready to pay the higher rate of interest can be accommodated – this will help somewhat. But in so far as this very willingness to be enterprising is checked by the higher rate, other remedies are necessary; for example, the diminished amount of private enterprise might be replaced by programmes of public development. But if I were to develop these ideas I should fall into controversial issues. This much, however, I can say. The more that everybody carries on as usual so far as all home business and home investment are concerned, and the less they allow themselves to be discouraged by the high Bank rate, the better it will be. One hopes, on the other hand, that the discouragement to loans to foreign countries will be as great as possible, and that investors will be reluctant, for the present, to subscribe to new loans to overseas. For the prime purpose of raising the Bank rate is, on this occasion, to diminish our foreign lending; and not as on some previous occasions, to damp down excessive optimism amongst business men at home.

I may sum up by saying that the direct consequences of a high Bank rate on foreign lending are likely to be efficacious in hindering the outward flow of gold. Nor is there any reason at all to expect immediate or sensational adverse developments in other directions. But the gradual and indirect consequences on business and other employment at home are likely to be serious – if no other measures are taken to counterbalance the discouragement of such very dear money. It lies outside my province to say why we find ourselves in these troubles – how far it is due to events outside this country over which we have no control, and how far they are the fruits of our own past policy.

Unemployment: A Discussion with Sir Josiah Stamp

[19 February 1930][1]

Kyenes's discussion with Sir Josiah Stamp, president of the London Midland and Scottish Railway, Director of the Bank of England, a member (with Keynes) of the Economic Ad visory Council, and a regular adviser to all inter-war British governments on economic affairs, required more preparation than most of his own talks. On the advice of Hilda Matheson, the two men went to great lengths to preserve a sense of spontaneity within a carefully timed structure.[2] As Keynes later wrote to Stamp[3]:

> You will remember that our method last time was to improvise a talk in the presence of a shorthand writer; then to correct the result and block out the

---

[1] *The Listener*, 26 February, 1930, 361–2; XX, 315–35.
[2] KCKP BR/1, Hilda Matheson to JMK, 29 January 1931.
[3] KCKP BR/2, JMK to J. Stamp, 12 December 1932.

40

general lines with cue words; and finally, to allow ourselves some fresh improvisation on the actual night within the general scheme.

KEYNES: Well, my dear Stamp, one talks in a vague way about there being something like one-and-a-half million unemployed men and women, but does that really give us a proper picture of the situation? How much unemployment is there actually?

STAMP: *No, Keynes, I do not think the bare figures are enough. There are all sorts of deceptive points about these figures. What I refer to particularly are the facts brought out by the Ministry of Labour, for example, that unemployment is mainly confined to a section of the population of about one-third of the whole. Two-thirds of the insured population, call it eleven-and-a-half millions, have been hardly touched by the problem since the War. These represent pretty stable employment mainly. Over a period of two-and-a-half years (tested) eight millions drew no unemployment pay at all. Call the one-third liable to unemployment three-and-a-half millions. Well, two-and-a-half millions of those in no single case had one hundred days in all unemployed over the period. Of course, for two-and-a-half millions to be subject or liable to seven weeks' unemployment in a year and to get into the 'million' as we call it, is in itself a pretty serious problem. So the second point is that it is not mainly a solid mass of unemployment. I believe that probably 50 per cent of those out of*

*work at any particular moment will be in work in a
month's time, but I cannot say how long for.*

KEYNES: I suppose from the human point of view
it helps a great deal that the unemployment
should be spread over a wide field and not all
concentrated on a few individuals. But does it
really affect the economic problem? Is it not
just as difficult to deal with 1,200,000 each
unemployed for a month as with 100,000 men
unemployed all the year round?

STAMP: *Well, yes, in a way, but it is very different in
certain important aspects. If unemployment comes
in a solid block over a long period you get disinte-
gration of character, the gradual destruction of the
morale, and what is more, you get a gradual loss of
personal skill with an economic loss. If it is carried
over short intervals then you have not those particular influences on character. It is a very different
problem if it is a shifting set of individuals and not
a solid block.*

KEYNES: After one has made every allowance for
unemployment of this transitory and comparatively harmless character, what would you estimate the abnormal volume of unemployment
as distinct from normal figures, which one must
probably expect even at the best of times?

STAMP: *Of course, it is only a guess, but looking at
the thing by and large I should think, in a country
made up as ours is, we are pretty certain to have
something like 300,000 to 400,000, even under the*

best conditions. The present problem is fluctuating between 600,000 and 700,000 and a million. Of course, it is going up rather rapidly as it is.

KEYNES: I will take your basis as an argument. Let us take the 400,000 men who will probably be unemployed at the best of times. At the present time the problem consists of something approaching one million men and women out of work, not necessarily always the same individuals, I grant you that, and not by any means equally spread over all trades and all parts of the country. Is not the figure of average productivity of British workmen, along with the plant and productive facilities, something like £200 a year?

STAMP: *Yes, that is about the figure; perhaps a trifle more.*

KEYNES: And what is it for a woman?

STAMP: *I do not think anybody has worked it out – something like £120 or £130.*

KEYNES: On the basis, then, of this million, we have got three-quarters of a million men who might be earning £200, and we have a quarter of a million women who might earn £120; that means that the average annual loss to the country, which you agree is abnormal, is something like £180,000,000. It is a shocking figure. Is it the sort of thing that happened before the War? I suppose it did, but only for short periods.

STAMP: *Yes.*

KEYNES: I suggest to you that the explanation is to be found partly in the much greater violence of the economic fluctuations which have been experienced in recent times. Even if one leaves out the years immediately after the War, when naturally conditions were quite abnormal, and thinks only of the years since, let us say, 1924, the fluctuations of a broad economic character have been enormously more violent than they were in the twenty-five years before the War.

STAMP: *I think there can be no doubt whatever that those economic bumps have been much more violent, but we have shown a remarkable power of actual absorption since the War – there are over a million more in employment. People are always talking of unemployment, but let us think for the moment of the people in employment. When you consider the broken and unstable conditions of industry, then it seems to me very much to the credit of Britain that we have been able to achieve this task of employing 150,000 more annually. The actual task of employing 150,000 more annually will gradually slow off because of the movement of the population. There will not be so many people entering into industry in excess of those going out in future. We are entering into a period where they more or less balance, and then it ought to be easier for the industrial machine to absorb this present block of one million.*

KEYNES: I do not think very much of that point. Population will probably go on increasing for at least five or six, if not ten, years more. Personally,

I do not think we should have diminished our unemployment to any great extent even if the population was already stationary.

STAMP: *I agree that in the main the problem is one of industrial balance, the specialised skill, with the specialised capital, particularly in your highly specialised export industries, and it is our dependence upon this that is really our trouble. You get that if you look at the distribution of unemployment – coal mining, steel and iron, engineering and shipbuilding accounting for quite the bulk of it, so you have a geographical as well as an industrial concentration. In seventy-one industries employment has grown by one-and-a-half millions, and in twenty-nine it has decreased by 650,000. The tendency is for expansion of business in the south – where unemployment is nothing like the same problem – and contraction of business in the north.*

KEYNES: While I think that economic fluctuations have been extraordinarily violent in recent years, I am afraid one has to admit there is also another reason besides economic fluctuation. The existence of the dole undoubtedly diminishes the pressure on the individual man to accept a rate of wages or a kind of employment which is not just what he wants or what he is used to. In the old days the pressure on the unemployed was to get back somehow or other into employment, and if that was so today surely it would have more effect on the prevailing rate of wages than it has today, so that the power of industry to absorb would be much greater than we have experienced. I cannot help feeling that we must partly attribute to the dole the extraordinary fact – at present it is an extraordinary fact – that, in spite of the fall in prices, and the fall in the cost of living, and the heavy unemployment, wages have practically not fallen at all since 1924.

STAMP: *I quite admit that the dole certainly has affected the old methods of economic adjustment. It has retarded things that acted automatically in the old days. For example, in the hard times there was the necessity for taking a lower wage in another job, or the necessity for moving about.*

KEYNES: I know that is one of the difficulties now, the housing conditions. If a man were in one district he could move his family to another district, but now he has to think twice before he moves because he may be disappointed; he may not find another house in the place he goes to.

STAMP: *I quite agree that housing has a very secondary influence on mobility, but do not let us labour this aspect too much. Do you not think from the workers' point of view there is something in this lack of the old freedom to adjust economic difficulties by the employer playing about with labour, moving it and reducing its reward? After all, if he can do that easily, then he has no need to do any thinking. It is only when the matter becomes really urgent that thinking is forced upon him. You really have to address yourself to all kinds of industrial waste, lack of up-to-date machinery and ineffective management. This may prove to be a blessing in disguise.*

KEYNES: I suppose that is always true of hard times. They do get rid of a lot of dead wood, but I have never been persuaded that that is a sufficient reason for having hard times. Besides, the position is still getting worse. Bowley,[4] the only man in this country outside Whitehall who really understands the unemployment figures, tells me that what alarms him about the immediate situation is that unemployment has not only definitely increased in recent weeks, but has spread to the miscellaneous industries, many of which were previously doing comparatively well. As a matter of fact, in coal mining, which we think of as a depressed industry, there is considerably less unemployment than there was a year ago, and owing to the mild weather the seasonal depression in building is very distinctly less. But in almost every other industry, without exception, the position is worse.

STAMP: *Yes, that is very interesting, but let me go back to the point you were making about the wonderful ease with which in the Victorian days we seemed to be able to absorb any difficulty and take it in our stride. We must not set as a standard of what is possible to us today exactly what we did in the*

---

[4] A. L. Bowley, Professor of Statistics in the University of London, 1919–36.

nineteenth century. For example, the accumulation of capital was on a pretty artificial basis during that period. I remember in an eloquent passage in one of your own books, in the preface, I think it was, you said that in that period men were tacitly allowed to make enormous fortunes if they turned them back into industry, so to speak, and prepared the way for greater produce in the next generation. By itself that is almost enough, but the fact that it is not done to anything like the same extent today means the almost entire slowing of industrial progress. Then, too, you had all those remarkable inventions which went to the root of industrial matters. I know we have wonderful inventions today, but perhaps not in increment comparable to those times.

Also you have not taken account of the fact that up to the War we had a very considerable relief to the growing population in emigration, which has been very largely cut off. You must give this age, stupid as it is and out of gear, some credit for the extraordinary difficulty that it has.

KEYNES: Well, it is not so surprising as you think it. I cannot see why there should be more difficulty in employing a population of 41,000,000 than 40,000,000. After all, we live by making things for one another.

STAMP: *I quite agree. Every new man is a potential customer of every other new man. It does not matter what the size of the population is, except with regard to the relation to assets. It is a question of the degree and speed with which the change takes place.*

It takes time for the new ones to be arranged as customers for each other.

KEYNES: But our population today is increasing much more slowly than it used to; indeed, I am not sure that our problem would not be easier if we were having a rapid increase of population. On the other hand, that rapid increase in the Victorian age was one of the things which kept business prosperous, when it paid employers to reduce wages. But none of these explanations seems to me to affect the main point in my mind. Is not the mere existence of general unemployment for any length of time an absurdity, a confession of failure, and a hopeless and inexcusable breakdown of the economic machine?

STAMP: *Your language is rather violent. You would not expect to put an earthquake tidy in a few minutes, would you? I object to the view that it is a confession of failure if you cannot put a complicated machine right all at once. I suppose that men are unemployed because no employer finds it worth while to employ them.*

KEYNES: I am not sure that that obvious remark helps us. If that is so, it must be because in many industries profits are low, or precarious, or non-existent. Why should that be so? Is it the difficulty of competing with lower wages abroad?

STAMP: *Well, when you come to consider the actual wages abroad – I do not mean monetary payments, but what wages will buy, the purchasing power of wages – when you think of those figures in France, Belgium and Germany you really wonder that things are not worse in this country than they are. Have you seen those figures published by the* International Labour Review? *They give them every quarter. Supposing you take an average wage in this country – what it will buy in commodities: bread, butter, cheese, shirts, boots, and everything – and call it 100, that is what the average wage-earner gets – 100 units of commodities. In Berlin he would get 73, in Italy 47, and in Paris even – wonderful, prosperous France – only 57.*

If that is the cost that is entering into the product, and the product is competing in a neutral market, you can see how extraordinarily difficult it is for a man paying a higher real wage to quote a competitive price.

KEYNES: Well, now, I think, we are getting on. What you are saying is that people are unemployed because wages are too high.

STAMP: *I would rather say that wages in some trades are higher than they ought to be in relation to others.*

KEYNES: Then there is the burden of social services. Have you got any figures about that?

STAMP: *That is a very important thing, too. I cannot give them exactly, but they are something like this: In 1911; a representative year before the War, the cost of social services – in a limited sense – was 14s. 6d. per head, whereas in 1928 it was 91s. 6d. But if you take in housing subsidies and education, then it was 32s. per head before the war and now*

150s., nearly five times as much. A good deal of it must be added to the cost of production. You can see that unless there has been a similar rise in other countries in competition with us – however efficient the social services may be – there is a serious handicap.

KEYNES: If I were a precisian I might say this is one more way of saying that wages are too high, but I do not want to press that point, because I do not think, any more than you do, that it is practicable to reduce wages, whether they are too high or not. Of course, if we are to avoid putting wages lower we must look round for some other method. What do we mean by all this talk about rationalisation if it is not an attempt to get efficient production per man up to the wage that is being paid?

STAMP: *But you must remember we have had against us all the time the run of prices, which is all against the business man; it makes him lose on stocks that he is holding; it has a bad tendency; the downward run of general prices is all against the business man.*

KEYNES: Yes, and in this country the fall of prices has been twice as great as elsewhere, because of the terms on which we returned to the gold standard. In my opinion the return to the gold standard in the way we did it set our currency system an almost impossible task, because we brought prices down without making any provision to bring costs of production down. This fall of prices all over the world is one of the most worrying things in the whole situation. If prices outside this country had been going up since 1925 that would have done something to balance the effect on this country of the return to the gold standard.

STAMP: *Hush, Maynard; I cannot bear it. Remember, I am a Director of the Bank of England.*

KEYNES: We will not say any more about that, but are there not other points? I do not believe that it is entirely foreign competition which is the trouble. Quite apart from this, I think that in our home affairs we are moving in a sort of vicious circle. The trouble is quite as much the lack of investment and enterprise at home. We are trying to invest abroad as much as we can, and our ability to do so leads to loss of gold, the Bank rate is raised, and credit is reduced. This discourages investment and enterprise at home, which leads to more unemployment and low profits. Indeed, profits have got so bad that many investors try to lend their money abroad preferably to at home, which leads to the loss of more gold, again a higher Bank rate, and we are in the vicious circle again.

STAMP: *I never can answer you when you are theorising, but is that what happens?*

KEYNES: To the best of my belief, yes. And that is not the only vicious circle we are revolving in. The low profits mean reduced yield of the taxes, so the taxes have to be raised, and that again reacts on the willingness to show enterprise and make new investments in this country. Personally, I believe one could do more for unemployment by some bold measure which would break this vicious circle than anything that one could hope from schemes of rationalisation. That is why I have been in favour for a good long time of a large programme of capital expenditure at home that would employ men and would give an outlet for our savings without putting pressure on the gold reserves of the Bank of England, as is bound to happen when the savings find their way abroad. Personally, I very much doubt, whatever we do, if we can revive our export industries to their old relative importance. Low wages and high tariffs abroad, keenness of international competition are too much for us. If that is so there is no way of reviving employment, except by increasing our investments at home.

STAMP: *Have you thought out the full implications of that? After all, what you suggest is really minimising the value of London and its financial importance in the world. I understand you would stop London being a free place for cheap foreign borrowing. After all, that foreign borrowing has been one of the most prominent factors of our export trade. The money is borrowed in London, which means that locomotives, iron, and steel are exported. You would let them go*

*to Paris or New York. In other words, you are after a
more self-contained Britain?*

KEYNES: No, not so. I am only saying we must adjust our habits to our circumstances.

STAMP: *You are certainly going to make foreign trade a
lesser proportion of the total trade.*

KEYNES: Yes. Well, we must, if our exports are too
dear in comparison with those abroad. I am
only concluding that our export trade being
less than it was, we must depend less on foreign
investment as an outlet for our savings. Also I
do not believe I am jeopardising the position of
London. It is much more dangerous for London
for us to endeavour to lend abroad beyond our
capacity. This is bound, in the long run, to
weaken our financial strength, to diminish our
gold reserves, and to make us a dear market.

STAMP: *My dear Maynard, you would suffer like any
other imperialistic Englishman, if India, Australia,
or South Africa wanted money for development –
say £10,000,000 – and you sent them off to New
York or Paris; and you forget those ancillary products of London's position in the foreign investment market we should lose, the value of many of
our shipping services and our insurance services
that have always followed the exports – always
followed the flag. You are becoming economically
more self-contained. I think you have got to realise
that those foreign ships bring food supplies to our
shores.*

KEYNES: I am all for encouraging these industries – shipping, or any of these things that we can have. I only say that, having expanded these industries as greatly as possible, we must then cut our investment coat to our cloth.

STAMP: *I suppose you have faced up to the fact that what in economic language we call the 'marginal return' for money at home is going to be less than for money abroad.*

KEYNES: Well, perhaps it is; but here are a million-and-a-half men doing nothing. If they could be put to work on anything moderately or reasonably useful, it would increase our national wealth. It ought not to be necessary to prove that the results of their labour would be worth five or six per cent per annum for ever. Is it not better that unemployed men should build a house, even if the house could only be let to yield three per cent on the investment? Some people seem to talk as though it were better to keep the men idle unless it could be proved for certain that the house could be let so as to yield five per cent. It is all a desperate muddle, in my opinion.

STAMP: *Would not part of the difficulty be met if we had cheaper money throughout the world?*

KEYNES: Well, perhaps; but I look upon it as being a choice between that and nothing, rather than between that and foreign investment, which is what you are suggesting. Perhaps it is inevitable.

STAMP: *It seems to me there is a tremendous amount in what you say, but it is a dangerous change for a densely populated country like ours to switch over.*

KEYNES: If we just sit tight there will be still more than a million men unemployed six months or a year hence. That is why I feel that a radical policy of some kind is worth trying, even if there are risks about it.

Saving and Spending

[14 January 1931][1]

Keynes returned to 'The Problem of Unemployment' as the second of four speakers in a series of that title. The other speakers were Henry Clay of the Bank of England, Alexander Loveday of the Financial and Economic Section of the League of Nations, and David Macgregor, the Drummond Professor of Political Economy at Oxford.

Keynes's talk was heard in Vienna by Friedrich Hayek who was about to come to England at the end of the month to visit Cambridge and then deliver a set of lectures at LSE under the title 'Prices and Production'. The talk infuriated Hayek 'who was very keen to fight Keynes' over the intellectual issues.[2] The conflict began during his visit to Cambridge, where he stayed with Dennis Robertson

---

[1] *The Listener*, 14 January 1931, 46–7; IX, 135–41 (title 'Saving and Spending').
[2] S. Howson, 'Keynes and the LSE Economists', *Journal of the History of Economic Thought*, XXI (September 2009), 265.

and continued in his London lectures and his two-part review of Keynes's recently published *A Treatise on Money*.[3]

The slump in trade and employment and the business losses which are being incurred are as bad as the worst which have ever occurred in the modern history of the world. No country is exempt. The privation and – what is sometimes worse – the anxiety which exist today in millions of homes all over the world is extreme. In the three chief industrial countries of the world, Great Britain, Germany and the United States, I estimate that probably 12 million industrial workers stand idle. But I am not sure that there is not even more human misery today in the great agricultural countries of the world – Canada, Australia, and South America, where millions of small farmers see themselves ruined by the fall in the prices of their products, so that their receipts after harvest bring them in much less than the crops have cost them to produce. For the fall in the prices of the great staple products of the world such as wheat, wool, sugar, cotton, and indeed most other commodities has been simply catastrophic. Most of these prices are now below their pre-war level; yet costs, as we all know, remain far above their pre-war

---

[3] 'Reflections on the Pure Theory of Money of Mr. J.M. Keynes', Part I, *Economica* XI (August 1931), 270–95; Part II, *Economica* XII (February 1932). 22–44.

level. A week or two ago, it is said, wheat in Liverpool sold at the lowest price recorded since the reign of Charles II more than 250 years ago. How is it possible for farmers to live in such conditions? Of course, it is impossible.

You might suppose – and some austere individuals do in fact believe – that cheapness must be an advantage, for what the producer loses, the consumer gains. But it is not so. For those of us who work – and we are in the great majority – can only consume so long as we produce. So that anything which interferes with the processes of production necessarily interferes also with those of consumption.

The reason for this is that there are all kinds of obstacles to the costs and prices of everything falling equally. For example, the wages costs of most manufacturers are practically the same as they were. See how the vicious process works out. The prices of wool and wheat fall. Good for the British consumer of wheat and woollen garments – so one might suppose. But the producers of wool and wheat, since they receive too little for their products, cannot make their usual purchases of British goods. Consequently, those British consumers who are at the same time workers who produce these goods find themselves out of work. What is the use of cheapness when incomes are falling?

When Dr Johnson, visiting the Island of Skye, was told that twenty eggs might be bought for a penny, he said, 'Sir, I don't gather from this that eggs are plenty in your miserable island, but that pence are few.'

Cheapness which is due to increased efficiency and skill in the arts of production is indeed a benefit. But cheapness which means the ruin of the producer is one of the greatest economic disasters which can possibly occur.

It would not be true to say that we are not taking a grave view of the case. Yet I doubt whether we are taking a grave enough view. In the enforced idleness of millions, enough potential wealth is running to waste to work wonders. Many million pounds' worth of goods could be produced each day by the workers and the plants which stand idle – and the workers would be the happier and the better for it. We ought to sit down to mend matters, in the mood of grave determination and the spirit of action at all costs, which we should have in a war. Yet a vast inertia seems to weigh us down. The peculiarity of the position today – to my mind – is that there is something to be said for nearly all the remedies that anyone has proposed, though some, of course, are better than others. All the rival policies have something to offer. Yet we adopt none of them.

The worst of it is that we have one excellent excuse for doing nothing. To a large extent the cure lies outside our own power. The problem is an international one, and for a country which depends on foreign trade as much as we do there are narrow limits to what we can achieve ourselves. But this is not the only reason why we are inactive. Nor is it a sufficient reason. For something we can do by ourselves. The other principal reason, in my opinion, is a serious misunderstanding as to what kind of action is useful and what kind is not. There are today many well-wishers of their country who believe that the most useful thing which they and their neighbours can do to mend the situation is to *save* more than usual. If they refrain from spending a larger proportion of their incomes than usual, they believe that they will have helped employment. If they are members of town or county councils, they believe that their right course at such a time as this is to oppose expenditure on new amenities or new public works.

Now, in certain circumstances all this would be quite right, but in present circumstances, unluckily, it is quite wrong. It is utterly harmful and misguided – the very opposite of the truth. For the object of saving is to release labour for employment on producing capital goods such as houses, factories, roads, machines, and the like. But if there is a large unemployed surplus already available for such purposes, then the effect of saving is merely to add to this surplus and therefore to increase the number of the unemployed. Moreover, when a man is thrown out of work in this or any other way, his diminished spending power causes further unemployment amongst those who would have produced what he can no longer afford to buy. And so the position gets worse and worse in a vicious circle.

The best guess I can make is that whenever you save five shillings, you put a man out of work for a day. Your saving that five shillings adds to unemployment to the extent of one man for one day – and so on in proportion. On the other hand, whenever you buy goods you increase employment – though they must be British, home-produced goods if you are to increase employment in this country. After all, this is only the plainest common sense. For if you buy goods, someone will have to make them. And if you do not buy goods, the shops will not clear their stocks, they will not give repeat orders, and someone will be thrown out of work.

Therefore, O patriotic housewives, sally out tomorrow early into the streets and go to the wonderful sales which are everywhere advertised. You will do yourselves good – for never were things so cheap, cheap beyond your dreams. Lay in a stock of household linen, of sheets and blankets to satisfy all your needs. And have the added joy that you are increasing employment, adding to the wealth of the country because you are setting on foot useful activities, bringing a chance and a hope to Lancashire, Yorkshire, and Belfast.

These are only examples. Do whatever is necessary to satisfy the most sensible needs of yourself and your household, make improvements, build.

For what we need now is not to button up our waistcoats tight, but to be in a mood of expansion, of activity – to do things, to buy things, to make things. Surely all this is the most obvious common sense. For take the extreme case. Suppose we were to stop spending our incomes altogether, and were to save the lot. Why, everyone would be out of work. And before long we should have no incomes to spend. No one would be a penny the richer, and the end would be that we should all starve to death – which would surely serve us right for refusing to buy things from one another, for refusing to take in one another's washing, since that is how we all live. The same is true, and even more so, of the work of a local authority. Now is the time for municipalities to be busy and active with all kinds of sensible improvements.

The patient does not need rest. He needs exercise. You cannot set men to work by holding back, by refusing to place orders, by inactivity. On the contrary, activity of one kind or another is the only possible means of making the wheels of economic progress and of the production of wealth go round again.

Nationally, too, I should like to see schemes of greatness and magnificence designed and carried through. I read a few days ago of a proposal to drive a great new road, a broad boulevard, parallel to the Strand, on the south side of the Thames, as a new thoroughfare joining Westminster to the City. That is the right sort of notion. But I should like to see something bigger still. For example, why not pull down the whole of South London from Westminster to Greenwich, and make a good job of it – housing on that convenient area near to their work a much greater population than at present, in far better buildings with all the conveniences of modern life, yet at the same time providing hundreds of acres of squares and avenues, parks and public spaces, having, when it was finished, something magnificent to the eye, yet useful and convenient to human life as a monument to our age. Would that employ men? Why, of course it would! Is it better that the men should stand idle and miserable, drawing the dole? Of course it is not.

These, then, are the chief observations which I want to leave with you now – first of all, to emphasise the extreme gravity of the situation, with about a quarter of our working population standing idle; next, that the trouble is a world-wide one which we cannot solve by ourselves; and, third, that we can all the same do something by ourselves and that something must take the form of activity, of doing things, of spending, of setting great enterprises afoot.

But I also have one final theme to put before you. I fancy that a reason why some people may be a little horrified at my suggestions is the fear that we are much too poor to be able to afford what they consider to be extravagance. They think that we are poor, much poorer than we were and that what we chiefly need is to cut our coat according to our cloth, by which they mean that we must curtail our consumption, reduce our standard of life, work harder and consume less; and that is the way out of the wood. This view is not, in my judgement, in accordance with the facts. We have plenty of cloth and only lack the courage to cut it into coats. I want, therefore, to give you some cheerful facts to dispose you to take an ampler view of the economic strength of this country.

Let me first remind you of the obvious. The great mass of the population is living much better than it ever lived before. We are supporting in idleness, at a higher standard of life than is possible for those who are in work in most other countries, nearly a quarter of our employable population. Yet at the same time the national wealth is increasing year by year. After paying wages which are far higher than, for example, those in France or Germany, after supporting a quarter of our population in idleness, after adding to the country's equipment of houses and roads and electrical plant and so forth on a substantial scale, we still have a surplus available to be lent to foreign countries, which in 1929 was greater than the surplus for such purposes of any other country in the world, even of the United States.

How do we do it? If the pessimists were right who believe that we are terribly inefficient, over-extravagant and getting poorer were right, obviously it would be impossible. We can only do it because the pessimists are quite wrong. We are not nearly so rich as we might be if we could manage our affairs better and not get them into such a muddle. But we are not inefficient, we are not poor, we are not living on our capital. Quite the contrary. Our labour and our plant are enormously more productive than they used to be. Our national income is going up quite quickly. That is how we do it.

Let me give you a few figures. As compared with so recent a date as 1924, our productive output per head has probably increased by 10 per cent. That is to say, we can produce the same amount of wealth with 10 per cent fewer men employed. As compared with pre-war the increase in output per head is probably as much as 20 per cent. Apart from changes in the value of money, the national income – even so recently as 1929 with a great mass of unemployment (it cannot, of course, be quite so good today) – was probably increasing by as much as £100 million a year; and this has been going on year by year for a good many years. At the same time we have been quietly carrying through almost a revolution in the distribution of incomes in the direction of equality.

Be confident, therefore, that we are suffering from the growing pains of youth, not from the rheumatics of old age. We are failing to make full use of our opportunities, failing to find an outlet for the great increase in our productive powers and our productive energy. Therefore we must not draw in our horns; we must push them out. Activity and boldness and enterprise, both individually and nationally, must be the cure.

The Slump

[12 April 1931][1]

Keynes followed Vincent Edgar Viscount D'Abernon, a financier and diplomat who had been British Ambassador to Germany between 1921 and 1926, and Sir Josiah Stamp in broadcasting on the American Columbia Broadcasting System.

This talk of mine follows on addresses from Sir Josiah Stamp and Lord D'Abernon. They have told you in different ways how the behaviour of the financial system and the banking system is capable of suddenly going off the rails, so to speak, and interfering with everyone's prosperity for obscure and complicated reasons which are difficult to understand and probably impossible to explain in a popular way. It is a matter which ought to be left to the experts. *They* ought to understand the machine. And *they* ought to be able to mend it

---

[1] XX, 515–20.

when it goes wrong. It is hopeless to expect the man in the street even to discover what is amiss; far less to put matters right. Unhappily, however, the machine is not well understood by anyone. In a sense there are no experts. Some of those representing themselves as such seem to me to talk much greater rubbish than an ordinary man could ever be capable of. And I daresay there are people – I am sure there are – who will say the same about me and my ideas. In other words, the science of economics, of banking, of finance is in a backward state. Yes, but I believe it is progressing very far all the same. Far enough, perhaps, to deal with the next slump. But I doubt whether the *present* one is going to be cured by these experts, if there are any, who really understand the machine, being asked in and allowed a free hand to mend it. We shall muddle along, just as we used to do when there was something wrong with our own insides, until time and nature and, perhaps, some happy accident work a cure by themselves.

The chances are at least two to one, more probably ten to one, that this is what we have to look forward to.

I should like, then, to use my time this afternoon to make a few observations about this prospect. And just as, when you are hearing an opera, you are prepared to believe for the time being that the voice of the tenor to whom you are listening comes from a golden-haired and god-like man with a spare and muscular figure, so, I beg you, persuade yourselves for the next quarter of an hour that the voice you are hearing is the voice of an expert.

Well, first of all, what a shameful and paradoxical thing it is that we should be suffering economic distress at all! Ten years ago when much the same thing happened, we had not so much reason to be surprised. For then it came as a natural reaction from a short-lived belief that we could ignore the effects of the War and live as though we had not been blowing our wealth away for several years. It was natural to believe that the slump of 1920–1 came as a reminder that we could not live as though the Great War and the unwise peace which followed it had never occurred. But today, ten years later, there can be no such excuse. We have accumulated far more material wealth than we have ever possessed before. The United States which has been building up its material possessions on an unparalleled scale is as hard hit as other countries which are not so wealthy. The improvement in manufacturing technique has been going on faster than ever before. Three men in a factory today can do on the average what before the war would have occupied four men. Moreover, agriculture and mining have not lagged behind. The power of the soil to render up its riches has been so vastly augmented by science and by organisation, that the improvement there is comparable with the improvements in the factory. In the United States and Western Europe, population has been increasing more slowly than formerly; so that we have not the same strain on our resources that we used to have in providing the newcomers with upbringing, houses and equipment.

Yet in the midst of this plenty – perhaps even because of it – we have millions of men standing idle, unable to earn a decent week's living. How can this be? It is not the engineers or the technicians who have failed us. It is – I venture to assert – nothing but a breakdown of the mysterious co-ordinating power of banking and finance. How shall I put it? This co-ordinating power has failed to co-ordinate. It has failed to create the environment in which our energies can find their appropriate outlet. We have produced our activities too far in certain directions compared with others. We have an unbalanced position. But this want of balance is not of a single character. It is not that we are making too many motor cars when we ought to be making more radio sets or more aeroplanes; or making too many agricultural machines when we ought to be making more machine tools; or building too many houses when we ought to be making more cars; or that we are growing too much wheat when we ought to be growing more corn or cotton; or that we are mining too much copper when we ought to be mining more lead. There appears to be a surplus capacity in every direction at once. How can that be? I believe that the explanation is, after all, simple; though I shall not be able to make it appear so. I believe that we are withholding from consumption a larger part of our incomes than is able to find an outlet in new constructive enterprises, or in anything which will serve to increase our accumulated capital. Or, as I like to express it, individuals may, as I have said, have to effect a tremendous change in the price of capital. These things do not happen easily or suddenly. From what I hear, I doubt if the people of the United States are yet appreciating the full gravity of the economic problem, with which they and the rest of the world are being faced.

III
Recovery

This section deals with various aspects of recovery policy, either in general or in particular countries. The final broadcast in this section shows Keynes's state of mind at the end of 1934, immediately before he began to circulate galley proofs of *The General Theory of Employment, Interest and Money* (1936) for comment.

State Planning

[14 March 1932][1]

This broadcast was part of a series on the state and industry.[2]

There is a new conception in the air today – a new conception of the possible functions of government; and in this discourse, the last but one of a series on the State and Industry, I must try to catch from the surrounding atmosphere, and re-deliver to it, what this new notion is.

It is called planning – state planning; something for which we had no accustomed English word even five years ago. It is not Socialism; it is not Communism. We can accept the desirability and even the necessity

---

[1] XI, 84–92.

[2] The reference on page 83 to 'the tragic death of Mr. Ivar Kreuger' referred to the suicide on 12 March of the Director of the firm Kreuger and Toll. After Kreuger's death widespread major irregularities in the firm's financial affairs were discovered. It was bankrupt.

of *planning* without being a Communist, a Socialist or a Fascist. But whether it is going to prove possible to carry out *planning* in actual practice without a great change in the traditions and in the machinery of democratic government – that is the big question mark. It is perhaps *the* problem of problems which the post-war generation of young Englishmen, who will be in the prime of life over the next twenty years, have to solve.

The forces which are driving the notion of planning into our heads are drawn from two distinct sources. The first is the force of example. The Russian Five-Year Plan has assaulted and captured the imagination of the world. This dream is not yet a realised success – it is much too soon to say that – but it is not the preposterous failure which many wise and experienced people expected it to be. We are now – as a reaction from our mistake – much more inclined, I think, to exaggerate its success than to underestimate it. We are ready to give Bolshevism the credit for much which is, in truth, the mystery and glamour and excitement, immemorial and eternal, of – not Communism – but Russia. Russia under Stalin or Lenin may be more like Russia under Nicholas or Alexander than either Russias are like England or Germany or the United States. Moreover, propaganda has produced its usual revulsion. We had been taught to think of Communism as involving so complete a destruction of human organisation, that when we learned that, after enormous sufferings and an incredible national effort of self-denial and the exercise of will, a Russian peasant can positively build a tractor of which the wheels go round and that there is a large electric power station at Leningrad, we gape with wonder and rush to the opposite conclusion that Communism is a roaring success.

And there is a second force of example – Italian Fascism which – attacking the same problem with an opposite mentality – seems to have saved Italy from chaos and to have established a modest level of material prosperity within a poor and over-populated country. Here again, when an Englishman learns that an Italian train has run to time, he gapes with wonder and is ready to accept the conclusion that Fascism is a roaring success.

For with our unmeasured arrogance, we judge the foreigner by a different and a lower standard. If the technical accomplishment of Austin or Morris or Courtauld had been achieved in Russia, if a Rolls Royce had been built in Moscow, if Sir Josiah Stamp had achieved in Siberia the reorganisation of the L[ondon] M[idland and] S[cottish] Railway, if the gold standard has been abandoned in an equal blaze of glory in some Fascist capital, then indeed we might have gaped. Thus our unmeasured national arrogance, which expects things to be done here, by whomsoever, with efficiency, but presumes that in Russia or in Italy there can be nothing but muddle, flatters the foreign experimentalists.

Nevertheless, let us not belittle these magnificent experiments or refuse to learn from them. For it is a remarkable and a significant thing that the two most extraordinary political movements of the modern age, approaching their task from opposite moral and emotional poles, should agree in this vital particular – that state planning, that intelligence and deliberation at the centre must supercede the admired disorder of the 19th century.

Nor are these forces of example the only forces which are driving our minds in this direction. There is also the failure of the unplanned economic systems of the world, of those where intelligent deliberation at the centre is minimised or rejected. Not indeed a relative failure; for England or the United States with a quarter of the population and a third of the productive plant at a standstill can nevertheless support a standard of life at least twice as high, I should suppose, as any existing Bolshevist or even Fascist state. But an absolute failure in relation to their own potentialities. That is what demands our attention. To establish a *prima facie* case for planning, we do not need to seek or discover success in the planned regimes to the south or to the east. It is sufficient to apprehend failure, as compared with opportunity, in the unplanned regimes here at home or to the west of the ocean.

For what are the economic events of the modern world which must most strike the apprehension of the dullest observer? The extraordinary capacity for the production of material wealth – though it were for the purposes of subsequent destruction – which we developed during the War; and the opposite picture today of starvation amidst plenty, our incredible inability to carry to our mouths the nourishment which we have produced with our hands. For the War was the nearest thing we have ever had in this country to a planned regime. The environment was unfavourable, the haste was excessive and hurried improvisations were inevitable. Yet it showed us the potentialities of modern technique to produce. On the other hand, today it is in the United States, where the national tradition is most antagonistic to the notion of planning and the forms of government least adapted to improvised planning, that the failure of the economic system, relatively to its opportunity, is most obvious.

Let us make a useful distinction. Let us mean by planning, or national economy, the problem of the *general* organisation of resources as distinct from the *particular* problems of production and distribution which are the province of the individual business technician and engineer. Now the business technician and the engineer, here and in the United States, have already carried their improvements to a point at which, if we could take full advantage of them, we should have gone far towards solving the problem of poverty altogether. Nor, in my judgement, is this failure to gather in and enjoy our harvest merely a phenomenon of the slump, of the violent periodic depression such as exists at this moment. It is at times of slump that the paradox of starving in the midst of potential plenty is most striking and outrageous. But I believe that we suffer a chronic failure to live up to the opportunities of our technical capacity to produce material goods.

To remedy this failure is the problem of planning. The problem of planning is to do those things which, from the nature of the case, is impossible for the individual to attempt. To bring in the collective intelligence, to find a place in the economic scheme of things for central deliberation is not to disparage the achievements of the individual mind or the initiative of the private person. Indeed it is the achievements of this initiative which have set the problem. It is the failure of the collective intelligence – I will not say to keep up with, but not to fall too disastrously behind – the achievements of the individual intelligence which we have to remedy. And we have to remedy it, if we can, without impairing the constructive energy of the individual mind, without hampering the liberty and the independence of the private person. If the England of the coming generations can solve that problem – and my proud patriotic heart harbours a hope that our national qualities may be best of all suited to do it – we shall have contributed, I think, something more valuable to civilisation than the Bolshevist or the Fascist can; though I do not overlook that each of these movements may be capable in its way of contributing something to the dignity of human nature which transcends the field and scale of operation that I attribute to national planning however complete and however successful.

I have said that it is of the essence of state planning to do those things which in the nature of the case lie outside the scope of the individual. It differs from Socialism and from Communism in that it does not seek to aggrandise the province of the state for its own sake. It does not aim at superceding the individual within the field of operations appropriate to the individual, or of transforming the wage system, or of abolishing the profit motive. Its object is to take hold of the central controls and to govern them with deliberate foresight and thus modify and condition the environment within which the individual freely operates with and against other individuals.

I will give you a few illustrations chosen both from the things which we pre-plan and from those which we might, and perhaps should, plan in future. The illustrations will not always be chosen for their intrinsic importance, but rather to convey to you just what is meant.

The distribution of the burden of taxation with a view to its effect on industry and on the divisions of incomes and of wealth is an example of state planning. A choice between rating relief and income tax relief, to take a specific instance, is an exercise in the problems of state planning. Tariffs can be a signal and outstanding example of planning. So is the control of the exchanges and the appropriate management of the value of sterling money in relation to the currencies of the rest of the world. So is the regulation of transport by road and by rail.

Or to take cases where we do not yet plan, or plan inadequately. Town planning and rural preservation is a good illustration, although it is only of a semi-economic character. For it is a case both where it is impossible for the individual to take the necessary action however much he may wish to do so, and where the benefit cannot possibly accrue to the individual even if he were to act. Yet it is a case where enormous benefits can accrue to the whole community both now and hereafter, if strong powers of central direction are assumed and employed.

Deliberate planning to influence the localisation of industry is a matter to which more attention is likely to be given before long. We are at present experiencing in this country a transfer of industry, socially most wasteful, from the industrial north to the London area, owing to lower rates and other advantages to the individual in the latter location. Yet the effect, of which the individual recks nothing, will be, if it is carried far, to waste enormous outlays in housing and municipal works in the older areas, outlays which are very large compared with the cost of the factories transferred.

The exercise of deliberate influence on the conditions and the environment which determine the rate of growth of population and of emigration and immigration is another matter of the greatest possible importance entirely outside the sphere of the individual, there the state must act if there is to be action at all.

But at such a time as the present the most out-standing opportunity for state planning throughout the world is to be found in the avoidance, or in the mitigation of industrial slumps during which there is so vast a loss of the world's potentialities for the creation of wealth. Here again we have a problem which lies completely outside the scope of the individual. The individual is helpless, – disastrously so, as there are abundant examples today, strewn upon the carpet of the world, to show. There is virtually nothing that he can do, however ardent his desire and however pressing his personal interest. He is swept along, together with all his fellows, on a flood which he cannot control or direct. And nothing can be of the least avail which does not come from concerted action at the centre.

We have a poignant example today of the helplessness of the individual, however powerful and however great his genius, in the tragic death of Mr Ivar Kreuger. Here was a man of perhaps the greatest constructive business intelligence of his age, a man whose far-flung activities have been in the widest sense in the public interest, who had conceived it his mission in the chaos of the post-war world to furnish a channel between the countries where resources were in surplus and those where they were desperately required, one who built on solid foundations and surrounded himself with such safeguards as could be humanly devised in the circumstances – suffering what the ignorant might mistake for the fate of the common gambler, but in truth crushed between the ice-bergs of a frozen world which no individual man could thaw and restore to the warmth of normal life. The spectacle of capitalists, striving to become liquid as it is politely called, that is to say pushing their friends and colleagues into the chilly stream, to be pushed in their turn by some yet more cautious fellow from behind, is not an edifying sight.

To my thinking – and here I am expressing what is only a personal view though, many are coming to share it – state planning, directed to the maintenance of the general average of industrial production and activity at the optimum level and to the abolition of unemployment, is at the same time the most important and the most difficult of the tasks before us. It will lead us, I believe, to far more deliberate and far-reaching policies of credit control, to a great preoccupation with the appropriate level of the rate of interest, and in general to an attempt to control the rate at which new investment is encouraged and facilitated to take place. It used to be believed that the level of interest and the rate of investment were self-regulatory, and needed no management and no planning; and that all would be for the best if natural forces were left to discover and establish the inner harmonies. But such a view does not square with the facts of experience. As I began by saying, it is the failure of the unplanned industrial world of Western Europe and America to regulate itself to the best advantage, or to reap the fruits of the genius of its scientists and its engineers and its business organisers, which is predisposing many persons to consider without prejudice those far-reaching experimental projects of the most constructive minds of the post-war world which go, conveniently, by the name of planning.

I am coming towards the end of my discourse. But there is one perplexing matter, upon which opinions differ, still to be mentioned. It may be desirable that we should be bolder and more ambitious in choosing the fields which we bring within the scope of state planning. But is it practicable in a democratic community? May it not be a necessary price to pay for the benefits of state planning, that we also suffer those other affronts to the individual which seem to be inseparable from a Bolshevist or a Fascist state? For myself, I do not see why this need be so. At least I should like to try whether it would be not possible to enjoy the advantages of both worlds. It is obvious that the task of state planning would be in many respects easier for an autocratic administration than for one dependent on parliamentary institutions and the breath of popular favour. On the other hand, the autocratic regime loses in two important respects: it loses that consciousness of consent to secure which is one of the principal arts of government and indeed of the conduct of all business, whether on a large scale or on a small; and except in its early years, when those rule who have carved their own way to power, all experience shows that it soon loses the capacity to select and to employ the best available and most disinterested talent.

Moreover, it should prove compatible with democratic and parliamentary government to introduce modern improvements and new organs of administration. Indeed this is surely most necessary, whether or not we greatly extend the existing functions of the state. State planning, as I conceive it, would not be administered or supervised in detail by democratically elected bodies. The latter would be judges, not of first, but of final instance, reserve forces to effect a change when grave mistakes had been made. The day-to-day tasks of state planning would be carried out in similiar way and with the same kind of instruments of administration under a democratic government, as they would be under an autocratic government. I contemplate nothing more than a further, and perhaps more conscious, step along the same path that we are already treading.

At any rate it is not unlikely that it will be along some such lines as this that English experiments will be made – not today perhaps, but tomorrow – with the object of solving the economic problems of the modern world. It may be that other countries will enjoy the rare opportunity of seeing three experiments carried on simultaneously, differing vastly on the surface yet each directed in effect to the solution of the same essential problem – the Five Year Plan in Russia; the Corporative state in Italy; and state planning by Public Corporations responsible to a democracy in Great Britain. And as lovers of our species, let us hope that they will *all* be successful.

Pros and Cons of Tariffs

[25 November 1932][1]

In June and July 1932, representatives from 19 countries met at Lausanne to discuss the future of reparations and war debt payments. The result of almost
a month's discussion was the end of reparations and
a decision to ask the League of Nations to call a
World Economic Conference the next year 'to decide
upon the measures to solve the other economic and
financial difficulties which are responsible for, and
may prolong, the present world crisis'. The conference was scheduled to open in London in June 1933.
In August 1932, Keynes became a member of
an Economic Advisory, Council Committee on
International Economic Policy, chaired by the
banker Sir Charles Addis, which had as its brief to
consider the programme of subjects to be discussed
at the forthcoming conference. In November, he
turned to one of the topics the Conference might

---

[1] *The Listener*, 30 November 1932, 769–70; XXI, 204–10.

discuss, opening a series of talks on free trade and protection.[2]

I do not know what claim I can have to be considered an impartial introducer to the partisans who are to follow me on this question of tariffs. We shall, all three of us, be trying to tell the truth. But I *can* claim that I have considerable sympathy with both parties; though, as you will find, I sympathise with both more from the practical than from the theoretical side. For the theoretical arguments which free traders and protectionists have each used are, many of them, as I think, invalid or misapplied. Each, on the other hand, has got hold of an important practical maxim.

The free trade position

Let me begin with the essential truth of the free trade position. It is best illustrated by beginning at home. We all know that, individually or taken by groups, we are much richer if we concentrate on those activities for which we are best fitted, become specialists in the production of certain articles, and live by exchanging our products for the products of other specialists. We do not doubt that we shall be richer if we concentrate industry in the towns. We know that it would be stupid to put a higher licence duty on a motor-car used in a county where it was

---

[2] The other speakers were Sir Henry Page-Croft (Conservative) and Clement Attlee (Labour), both M.P.s.

not manufactured. It never occurs to us to put on special taxes designed to prevent a Lancashire man from using a car made in Birmingham. And all this is just as true between countries, as it is between individuals or between districts. It is a waste and a stupidity for us to make one thing inefficiently when we might be better employed making something else. There is no mysterious quality in a frontier which upsets this obvious conclusion of common sense. Most protectionist arguments to the contrary are sophistries – particularly the one which contends that what I have been saying holds good under universal free trade, and that, if other countries impose tariffs, it becomes advantageous to us to do the same. The tariffs of the foreigner reduce the opportunities for advantageous trade; but that is no reason why *we* should reduce them still further. Moreover, if we have to pay more than we need for what we use, that will raise our costs even in those branches of production for which we are best suited; so that our efficiency will go downhill all along the line.

All this is, surely, obvious; but that does not make it unimportant. On the contrary, it is frightfully important. The free trader starts with an enormous presumption in his favour. Nine times out of ten he is speaking forth the words of wisdom and simple truth – of peace and of good will also–against some little fellow who is trying by sophistry and sometimes by corruption to sneak an advantage for himself at the expense of his neighbour and his country. The free trader walks erect in the light of day, speaking all passers-by fair and friendly, while the protectionist is snarling in his corner.

Disappointment with Ottawa

Nor does practical experience of tariffs in the least modify this general presumption. Quite the contrary. There is no important country with an old established tariff system which has not committed a hundred stupidities – stupidities difficult to reverse, once done, without doing a further injury – stupidities frankly confessed by all understanding people within the country itself. We ourselves, in my judgement, have just had an example of this in the outcome of the Ottawa Conference. For, in spite of the high hopes and high ideals with which this conference was entered upon, it is difficult to see how the warmest advocates of economic co-operation within the Empire can regard it otherwise than as a disappointment – even apart from the difficulties which it may put in the way of achieving something useful at the World Economic Conference to be held next spring. It is a good example of how the worse elements in tariff bargaining tend to overcome the better elements, when it comes to business. Instead of promoting freer trade by genuine tariff reductions within the Empire, as Mr Baldwin in his opening address hoped that it would, I personally am of the opinion that it has riveted tariffs more firmly than before on all concerned – though some authorities, I know, are prepared to maintain the contrary.

The limitations of free trade

Why, then, did I begin by saying that I sympathised with both sides? I will tell you. In spite of all that I have just said, there are some important respects in which those who are not afraid to use tariffs have a broader conception of the national economic life and a truer feeling for the quality of it. Free traders, fortified into presumption by the essential truths – one might say truisms – of their cause, have greatly overvalued the social advantage of mere market cheapness, and have attributed excellences which do not exist to the mere operation of the methods of *laissez-faire*. The protectionist has often used bad economic arguments, but he has sometimes had a truer sense of the complicated balances and harmonies and qualities of a sound national economic life, and of the wisdom of not unduly sacrificing any part even to the whole. The virtues of variety and universality, the opportunity for the use of every gift and every aptitude, the amenities of life, the old established traditions of a countryside – all those things, of which there are many, even in the material life of a country, which money cannot buy, need to be considered. National protection has its idealistic side, too – a side which a well-balanced national economic policy will try to marry with the peace and truth and international fair-dealing of free trade.

If it were true that we should be a little richer, provided that the whole country and all the workers in it were to specialise on half-a-dozen mass-produced

products, each individual doing nothing and having
no hopes of doing anything except one minute,
unskilled, repetitive act all his life long, should we
all cry out for the immediate destruction of the end-
less variety of trades and crafts and employments
which stand in the way of the glorious attainment of
this maximum degree of specialised cheapness? Of
course we should not – and that is enough to prove
that the case for free trade, as I began by stating it,
has left something out. Our task is to redress the balance of the argument.

Tariffs and employment

I will give three examples. But before I come to them,
there is a further concession to be made to the protectionist case. There was a time when I denied the
temporary usefulness of a tariff as a means of com-
bating unemployment. I still think that a world wide
system of tariffs will increase unemployment rather
than diminish it, in the world as a whole. But I should
now admit that if we put on a tariff at a time of severe
unemployment it would be likely to shift on to other
countries some part of our own burden of unemployment. For the free trade argument against the
use of a tariff for drawing workers into an industry
for which they are relatively ill-suited fundamentally
assumes that, in the absence of a tariff, they will be
employed in some other more suitable industry, and
does not allow for the contingency that they may
not be employed at all.

Protection for motor-cars

Now for my examples of tariffs which I deem to be justified. First, our motor-car industry. I have always maintained that the protection which we have accorded to this industry every since the War was wise and beneficial. This was a new, progressive, ever-changing industry of first-class interest and importance in itself, of a kind for which one would expect our national aptitudes to be excellent, offering highly congenial and attractive tasks and problems to one typical kind of Englishman. Indeed, it would be a shocking thing if we were to be without a prosperous and inventive motor industry. But during the War, when we were otherwise occupied, the United States had gained a great start on us both financially and technically; so that it was certain that the English industry would be bankrupt before it could pay, if it were to be exposed to the full force of foreign competition. The results today are a triumphant vindication of the protection we gave to it. Can anyone deny it?

For iron and steel

That is a new industry. My next example is an old one – iron and steel. Here is a case of an industry with a great past, languishing to decay – by our own fault, in no small degree. The problem is intricate – I cannot enter upon it here. But I should not discard the assistance of a tariff if it were part of a well-concerted general scheme for the regeneration of the industry. For I am convinced that this is an industry for which, if one thinks in decades and not in single years, we are singularly well adapted. Yet it is obvious that much lasting injury can be done to it in a short time. Its further debilitation will devastate whole neighbourhoods; it will root up tens of thousands of men from their homes and associations to throw them helpless on the world; and it will render valueless miles of houses the financial fortunes of which the steel plants cannot take into account in their calculations of what will or will not pay. I do not consider it important, over against this, that steel today should be as cheap as possible to the consumer. I wish to see the blast furnaces of the north-east coast roar again and ships of British steel sail out of the Clyde. And I am prepared, if necessary, to pay a little for the satisfaction.

And for agriculture

My last example is the greatest crux of all for the uncompromising free trader – agriculture. Suppose it to be true that the average farmer in this country will be ruined unless the prices of his output are raised by taxes on food or equivalent measures. Is the free trader prepared to say – Well, let farming go? Of course we must not be foolish in our remedies, or attract the farmer into crops for which the country is unsuited compared with other crops. But that is not the dilemma I am putting to the free trader. Suppose that it is not possible for British farming today, so

long as it is exposed to the uncertainties of unre-
stricted competition, to provide for those employed
in it the standard of life set by the mass-produced
industries of the towns – and this supposition is by
no means improbable. Are there any free traders who
say – Well, let farming go? I hope there are none
such. For, anyone who does not imprison his mind
in a strait-jacket, must know, as well as you and I do,
that the pursuit of agriculture is part of a complete
national life. I said above that a prosperous motor
industry was a national necessity, if only given an
opening to one kind of typical Englishman. It is true
in the same way that another kind needs as his pursuit in life the care and breeding of domestic animals
and contact with the changing seasons and the soil.
To say that the country cannot afford agriculture is
to delude oneself about the meaning of the word
'afford'. A country which cannot afford art or agriculture, invention or tradition is a country in which
one cannot afford to live.

The path of wisdom in these matters is, then, a
narrow one, to be trodden safely only by those who
see the pitfalls on both sides. Neither free trade nor
protection can present a theoretical case which
entitles it to claim supremacy in practice. Protection
is a dangerous and expensive method of redressing
a want of balance and security in a nation's economic life. But there are times when we cannot
safely trust ourselves to the blindness of economic
forces; and when no alternative weapon as efficacious as tariffs lies ready to our hand.

Spending and Saving: A Discussion with Sir Josiah Stamp

[4 January 1933][1]

On 9 November 1932, Charles Siepmann, Hilda Matheson's successor as Director of Talks, approached Keynes with the idea of having a discussion on the question of saving and spending and suggested that Lionel Robbins, Professor of Economics at LSE, be asked to take the opposite point of view. Keynes was attracted by the idea of a discussion, but he continued[2]

I do rather hesitate about taking it on with Robbins as my colleague. He is so difficult and queer! and his reasons for differing are so eccentric and so totally different from the ordinary man's, that it

---

[1] *The Listener*, 11 January 1933; XXI, 145–54.
[2] KCKP, BR/2, C. Siepmann to JMK, 9 November 1932.

might be difficult to bring out the real points that are perplexing the public.[3]

Siepmann reported that he had already written to Robbins, who had not replied, but that he would 'wiggle out if he could'.[4] Keynes replied suggesting two alternative approaches to the talk.[5]

> One way would be to make it a discussion between two people who did not differ fundamentally, but were disposed to stress one side or another. On the whole I think that this would be by far the most effective and interesting, and also the most sensible. If that idea attracts you, then I am sure that we ought to try Stamp again. ...
>
> The other method would be to have more of a hammer and tongs debate, each side trying to make a bit of an ass of the other. For this I have no equally good suggestion to make.

When Stamp agreed to appear with Keynes, the latter suggested that they repeat their earlier procedure (above 40–1). Stamp agreed and also suggested that they create the atmosphere of 'a *discussion* rather than a debate' and spend the first half consolidating

---

[3] KCKP, BR/2, JMK to C. Siepmann, 10 November 1932. Keynes was referring to Robbins's then attachment to the Austrian theories of the business cycle held by his friend and colleague Friedrich Hayek.

[4] KCKP, BR/2, C. Siepmann to JMK, 11 November, 1932. The letter contained a P.S. that Robbins was off.

[5] KCKP, BR/2, JMK to C. Siepmann, 15 November 1932.

the areas of agreement before going on to points of difference.[6]

> STAMP: *It is a long time, Keynes, since we have had such a chance for a really confidential chat about things, and many a day since I taught you anything. Now, we've been reading all this in the papers about spending and saving, getting mixed up in it ourselves, I suppose. Where do you think the public have got to on the subject? Has all this discussion really brought out any special points and made them clear, or is it all just as confused as when it first began?*
>
> KEYNES: It's my impression that the public mood is changing. There was a good deal of panic about a year ago, but today isn't it getting realised pretty generally that one man's expenditure is another man's income? At any rate, that seems to me to be the central truth, never to be forgotten. Whenever anyone cuts down expenditure, whether as an individual or a town council or a Government Department, next morning someone for sure finds that his income has been cut off, and that is not the end of the story. The fellow who wakes up to find that his income is reduced or that he is thrown out of work by that particular piece of economy is compelled in his turn to cut down his expenditure, whether he wants to or not.

---

[6] KCKP, BR/2, J. Stamp to JMK, 13 December 1932.

STAMP: *That means he is cutting down the second man's income, and that is another man out of work.*

KEYNES: Yes, that is the mischief. Once the rot has started, it is most difficult to stop.

STAMP: *Just a minute. Let us first look at the Department or individual economising, and consider the result of the action. A country or a town, just like an individual, must live within its resources, and it will get into grave difficulties if it tries to go beyond them, for very soon it will be living on its capital.*

KEYNES: There can only be one object in economy, namely, to substitute some other better and wiser piece of expenditure for it.

STAMP: *Substitute! Yes, that brings me to my point. For example, what if the Government or the local authority economised in order to relieve taxation or rates, and allowed the individuals to spend more; or if the individuals spent less on consumption, in order that they or other people to whom they lent their money might build houses or factories. Wouldn't that get things right?*

KEYNES: But, my dear Stamp, is that what's happening? I suspect that the authorities are often economising without reducing rates or taxes and passing the extra spending power to the individual, and even when the individual has been given the extra spending power he is often playing for safety, or at least he thinks it virtuous to save and not to spend. But, as a matter of fact, it is not really these economies which will relieve the rates or taxes that I am making trouble about. It is that form of economy which means cutting off expenditure, which would naturally be met by borrowing. For in that case there is no advantage in the taxpayer having more, to compensate the loss of income for the fellow who has been retrenched.

STAMP: *Then what we really mean is that unless the public expenditure which is cut off is balanced by additional personal expenditure, there will be too much saving. After all, normal saving is only a different kind of expenditure, passed on to some public authority or business for producing bricks and machinery. Saving means more bricks; spending means more boots.*

KEYNES: Yes, that's the whole point. Unless someone is using capital in bricks or the like, the country's productive resources are wasted, and saving is no longer another kind of spending. That's why I say that the deliberate curtailment of normal useful developments, which would ordinarily be met out of borrowing, seems to me to be, in present circumstances, a crazy as well as an injurious policy.

STAMP: *The difficulty is to find what you call 'normal useful developments'.*

KEYNES: On the contrary. The Ministry of Health, if I am rightly informed, is turning down practically all the normal applications of local authorities to borrow. I read, for instance, in a paper – I cannot vouch for the figures myself – that a questionnaire issued to the Building Industry National Council shows that something like £30,000,000 worth of public works have been held up as a result of the national economy campaign. National campaign for the intensification of unemployment is what I should call it!

STAMP: *Why on earth have they carried it to those limits? Why are they doing it?*

KEYNES: I cannot imagine. It's probably a legacy of some panic decision made many months ago, which someone has forgotten to reverse. Think what it would mean to the spirit of the nation, and in human terms, if we had even another quarter of a million employed. And I wouldn't be at all sure that the repercussions would stop there.

STAMP: *I am rather tender about Government Departments. Anyway, ragging a Government Department, whether it deserves it or not, is quite a different thing from urging individuals to spend more. Surely that might be both rather foolish and rather dangerous: foolish because of the reduction in their incomes, spending more than they can really afford; dangerous because if you once encourage people to be reckless and to break down habits of thrift, you don't know where it will end.*

KEYNES: I quite agree. It is not the individual who is the sinner, and therefore it is not reasonable to expect that it is from individual action that the remedy can come. That is why I stress so much the policy of public authorities. It is they who must start the ball rolling. You cannot expect individuals to spend much more when they are already, some of them, getting into debt. You cannot expect business men to launch out into extensions while they are making losses. It is the organised community which must find wise ways of spending to start the ball rolling.

STAMP: *I will put my point the other way round. Isn't the importance of keeping up habits of thrift in the individual an extra reason why public authorities should feel their responsibilities in this respect? If these habits and methods of thrift and saving, which are so useful in individual life, are to be made beneficial to the community, then it is absolutely essential to find useful ways of using the money which they are saving.*

KEYNES: Yes, that is my point. Besides, isn't curtailment of activities, and therefore of the national income, an incredibly short-sighted way of trying to balance the Budget?

STAMP: *Well, apart from any far-reaching questions of national credit, it would seem to me that all of it hits the Chancellor of the Exchequer in two ways. First of all, he has to meet the unemployment benefit for the men thrown out of work, and then, again, the yield of his taxes falls away, because he has to depend either on a man's income or on his expenditure, in two kinds of taxes. So that anything which reduces both the income and the expenditure of the individual must diminish the yield of the taxes.*

And, of course, if you are going to have losses on the receipt side and more on the payment side of the Budget, how would you remedy it, because an unbalanced Budget destroys our credit? Of course, I know there is a difference between the normal and the abnormal period.

KEYNES: But, Stamp, you will never balance the Budget through measures which reduce the national income. The Chancellor would simply be chasing his own tail – or cloven hoof! The only chance of balancing the Budget in the long run is to bring things back to normal, and so avoid the enormous Budget charges arising out of unemployment. So I contend that, even if you take the Budget as your test, the criterion of whether the economy would be useful is the state of employment. In a war, for example, everyone is busy, and it is difficult to get important and necessary jobs carried out, which is an obvious indication that if one kind of expenditure is reduced, an alternative and wiser expenditure will take its place.

STAMP: *The same would apply if the Government has a great housing scheme or a slum clearance scheme.*

KEYNES: Yes, or additional railways. Or new land which might be drained, or industries expanded rapidly owing to some new invention, or any such reason as that.

STAMP: *But if, as today, a half of the labour and plant of the country are idle, that is an indication that if one kind of expenditure is reduced it will not be replaced by an alternative and wiser expenditure. It means that nothing will take its place: no one will be richer, and everyone will be poorer.*

KEYNES: I find we agree more than we thought, but many a man considers even plausible expenditure today as truly daft. When the county council builds houses, the country will be richer [even] if the houses yield no rent at all. If it does not build houses, we shall just have nothing to show for it except more men on the dole.

STAMP: *Always, provided that you pay a reasonable regard to people's ideas about public credit. It is not going to do any government or other authority any good if it is supposed to be heading for bankruptcy.*

KEYNES: I do not believe that measures which truly enrich the country will injure the public credit. You have forgotten my point that it is the burden of unemployment and the decline in the national income which are upsetting the Budget. Look after the unemployment, and the Budget will look after itself.

STAMP: *So much for the public expenditure side of the case. What about developing the outlets for individual savings? These savings have to go on if each man is to be reasonably prudent in his own way of living. What outlets do you approve of yourself, and what new ways can you suggest?*

KEYNES: Let me give you an example of the sort of thing which seems to me to be wholly admirable. The building societies have done splendid work since the War, because they have organised saving on the one hand, and have at the same time organised ways of using the thrift on building houses on the other hand. To them the two complementary activities have gone hand in hand. Are they not even in danger of attracting more funds than they can use?

STAMP: *I won't comment on that, except to say you make me feel virtuous. But I hope you won't draw from their case the conclusion that a movement, say, like the National Savings Certificate movement, ought to be discarded.*

KEYNES: Stamp, you are thinking of our broadcast a year or so ago [above 41–56]. I have been much misunderstood about that. Diminished saving for the class of people who buy savings certificates I reckon a very second-rate remedy. My argument was that if public works are stopped, particularly at a time when private enterprise is stopping from temporary overcapacity and is therefore not in a position to expand, then private saving can do any amount of harm. You remember what I said – every pound saved puts a man out of work. I still maintain that, and I doubt if you will deny it.

STAMP: *No, certainly, if nothing is going to be done with the resources which are released, people will have stinted themselves of something useful or pleasant with no other result than that of putting out of work the man who would have worked to provide for them. You mustn't conclude from this that private spending is the remedy that I prefer.*

KEYNES: On the contrary. I only put forward private spending as a way in which well-disposed individuals could undo a little of the harm which the Government is doing by curtailing the work which we ought to set going as an organised community. In my opinion, it isn't really the business of private individuals to spend more than they naturally would, any more than it is their business to provide for the unemployed by private charity. These things should be done by the organised community as a whole – that is to say, by public authorities.

STAMP: *I am very glad that I have got you to clear that up, because I don't think many people have really understood that this is the line you intended to take. I am glad you don't take an objection to private thrift, for whatever benefits you might get today along that line, you would be doing vastly more mischief in the long run, I feel.*

KEYNES: Certainly, I even save myself at times. I am its friend by demanding a policy which would allow thrift to be useful and productive to the community. The enemies of thrift are those who, by cutting off the outlets for it, deprive it of its purpose, and turn what should be a public benefit into an instrument for the aggravation of unemployment. That, I repeat, is what it is in this sort of circumstances. If you cut off the demand from the county council and public authorities, there isn't slightest chance that a private domestic business alone will be able to use anything approaching the amount which a healthy and well-employed community of England would save, believing in the principle of thrift.

STAMP: *Aren't you being rather pessimistic about the amount of unemployment which expanding private enterprise might absorb, and have you looked at the thing from the point of view of statistics of saving in the past? Don't you think that with a real revival of business there might be a more remarkable absorption of these savings than we are at present inclined to think?*

KEYNES: I doubt it. You must take into account the embargo which is now in force against a great deal of the foreign lending, which used to get a big proportion of our savings. We have got to replace all that, you know. I doubt if private enterprise at home, even in its palmiest days, ever absorbed half the national savings, and considering the extent to which public utilities are in public hands today, I am sure that they never will in the future. I am all for giving private enterprise a run, and using all the capital it can, but I believe one is living in a false paradise if one supposes that in any foreseeable future it will be able to take up the amount which this country could save when it was prosperous and everybody properly employed.

STAMP: *I believe that that way of looking at it hasn't been faced up to by many people. What about the statistical attitude to it? Savings come to a certain figure. They are bound to, with all the different opportunities for saving – insurance and the like – that ought to go on, and if any individual, being reasonably prudent in his own living, raises the figure, it must be properly used by business expansion or public expenditure, or the two put together, and if these two don't do the trick then there is serious trouble with employment. If there is a gap, then the best thing is for business to expand to fill it up. Failing this, then the next best thing is for public expenditure to increase and fill it up. If both of these fail, or for any good reason the public expenditure cannot be increased enough, then the final device or makeshift to get the two sides to balance is for the savings themselves to be decreased until the excess above the two uses has disappeared, but somehow or other the difference must be used or made to disappear.*

KEYNES: Yes, and I repeat that it won't be by business. In the near future you won't find business expansion in this country anything like enough to absorb the savings. Expenditure from various public authorities and public boards and so on must be increased, or if people won't have that, then the alternative has to be adopted of reducing savings. You can't have it both ways.

STAMP: *I go a long way with you in this direction, but I beg you not to treat too lightly the principle of unwise and unbalanced public budgets. That kind of principle must still be respected. I believe that the true nature of our dilemma is the fact that one principle*

*cannot always walk alone in life, and two principles,
each one excellent in itself, may sometimes conflict.
We are forced to prefer one to the other at any given
time. We know the virtuous person says two things.
First, thrift is a fine thing; save all you can. He also
says, to reduce public expenditure is bad, cut it out.
He doesn't realise that if each of these highly virtuous principles is carried to an extreme, there must
be a serious alteration to the equilibrium of savings,
so that they are used as a kind of mechanical necessity or virtue in our modern economical scheme,
while the views about balanced budgets are a kind
of psychological necessity.*

KEYNES: You are always going back to this question of the Budget. So far as that is concerned,
I should say that things like the sinking fund
aren't so important in these days as they would
be in more prosperous times, and I think that
the Chancellor of the Exchequer would be long-
sighted if he were to take rather an optimistic
view, and give us perhaps in his next Budget
rather more relief than is strictly justified by the
facts actually in sight. If he does, he will help
to bring the facts in sight, which would justify
the optimism that he has adopted. But that is
not really what I want. It is loan expenditure I
am wanting. It is all those capital developments
of varying utility. I agree that traditionally we
think it quite proper to finance all the means
by loans, and that expenditure of that kind is
carried out by local authorities or by the central

government. And I believe that in the long run a policy of that kind would really help the Budget, more than will the other policy, of trying to cut things down and down.

STAMP: *What you are saying really is that at times when business expansion is at a low point people are not launching out, but it is rather at these times that public expansion ought to be at its height. No mention of banks or rate of interest or monetary value! Marvellous! I think we will agree that it is no easy thing to find an outlet for our savings at the present time, and therefore I am with you that we should not neglect any opportunity which offers itself. There are a thousand things which need doing if we are to be a community equipped in proportion to our opportunities, taking advantage of all modern scientific developments. We get rich by doing things, and not by cutting off activities. So up, and be busy.*

KEYNES: Yes, the fact is that spending and saving are in very truth complementary activities. The object of saving is to spend the proceeds on useful and necessary equipment. We must save in order that spending may be healthy, and equally we must spend if saving is to be healthy.

STAMP: *In short, this saving and spending of ours are really, or ought to be, sort of sister shows.*

The World Economic Conference: A Conversation with Walter Lippmann

[11 June 1933][1]

The World Economic Conference was to open on 12 June 1933. On the eve of the Conference, Keynes joined Walter Lippmann, the American journalist and author whom he had known since 1919, in a transatlantic conversation. Initially, Keynes had hoped that he might replicate the method of preparation that he had used with Josiah Stamp, but Lippmann was too busy and they put the programme together by exchanging cabled extracts which they read.

LIPPMANN: *With what expectations are you in London welcoming the delegates to the great Conference which begins tomorrow?*

---

[1] *The Listener*, 14 June 1933; XXI, 251–9.

KEYNES: With mingled hopes and doubts. Sixty-six nations are assembling: statesmen and financiers arrive by every train. The world's needs are desperate: we have, all of us, mismanaged our affairs, we live miserably in a world of the greatest potential wealth. And we are wondering, at last, whether anything is to be hoped from collective wisdom. But we are wondering a little dismally. For is there anything in the world to which six nations are likely to agree, let alone sixty-six? We have had experience of conferences since the War, and we know that it will be extraordinarily difficult to avoid a fiasco. Every previous conference of the kind has ended in empty platitudes and ambiguous phrases so boring and vapid that they have expired in a universal yawn. Isn't the present shocking state of the world partly due to the lack of imagination which they have shown, or sincere constructiveness or readiness for that reasonable give and take which is the basis of all decent human relations? Isn't there every reason to fear that this Conference will be just as bad? For my part I put all my hopes on one possibility – that England and America should somehow find a way to get together on an agreed programme – to do, in fact, just what we failed to do in Paris in 1919. For there are few remedies which we could not apply, acting together, even if others were to hold back.

I am sure that we shall want to fall in with your plans to the best of our ability. But so far we really don't know what your policy is. Your President has persuaded Congress to provide him with some lovely blank sheets of writing paper and some beautifully sharp pencils, but what part of his powers he really means to rely on, we, over here, simply don't know. For me, however, the outstanding fact is that President Roosevelt seems more willing than most of those in authority in the world to have some kind of bold and constructive policy commensurate with our necessities. Whether I should think his policy the ideal one if I knew in detail just what it is, I am not certain. But I do feel some confidence that it is of a right tendency. Tell me, along what lines, in your opinion, is a common policy most practicable?

LIPPMANN: *I agree with you that great assemblages of delegates from all parts of the earth don't usually make definite and constructive decisions. And so I agree, too, that we have to approach this Conference differently from the many conferences which have preceded it. Thus, for example, we ought not, I think, to look forward to the writing of an elaborate treaty which has to be agreed upon by some sixty-six national delegations and then ratified or rejected by some sixty[-six] legislative bodies. This Conference is not like the Disarmament Conference, for example, where no nation can act except in relation to all other nations. Many of us over here believe that the governments, particularly in the large nations, have the power to combat the depression without waiting for universal agreement at London on the measures that they are to take. In fact, we believe that only as the principal countries are prepared to deal as boldly with the depression within their boundaries as the Roosevelt Administration is dealing with it inside the United States, is there much likelihood of international agreement on such matters as the reconstruction of the world monetary standard and the reduction of trade barriers. In other words, we believe that before the Conference can hope to make real progress with the problems which it has to discuss, the chief financial and commercial nations – Great Britain, France and the United States – must use their own enormous power to raise prices, to relieve debtors and the unemployed and generally to enhance the capacity of their own people to buy goods. The strongest nations must use the powers under their control to lead the way out of the depression. I gather that that is what you have in mind. If so, I heartily agree with it and I believe it represents the dominant view of the American people. The strong nations must lead. International agreements will follow such action. They can hardly precede it. For most of the subjects which are to be discussed in London – the instability of the exchanges, the super tariffs, the hoarding of gold by central banks and by governments – are consequences of the depression and will not be remedied until the depression itself begins to clear up.*

If we take this view of the matter, it would follow that in the first and most important phase of the

*discussion, the problem as between Great Britain
and the United States is not a question of matching
divergent national interests and of attempting to
strike a bargain. Our task is to persuade and encourage one another to act along parallel lines. Both
countries, for example, have been revaluing their
currencies in terms of gold – Great Britain since
September 1931, the United States since April, 1933.
Both countries have been forced to do this for essentially the same reason, namely, that the exorbitant
rise in the value of gold made fixed charges in terms
of gold socially and politically intolerable to their
own peoples. Now, this process of revaluation in
terms of gold is not, or at least ought not to be, in
my opinion, a matter of trying to gain temporary
advantages in international trade. For the United
States, certainly, it is a matter of restoring some kind
of workable balance between prices, debts, wages,
fixed charges and profits. Therefore, if we are clear
about our purposes, we shall not be concerned about
where the dollar is ultimately stabilised in relation
to the pound. Our first concern will be where the
dollar is stabilised in relation to commodities in the
American market. Our second concern will be
whether and where the dollar can also be stabilised
in relation to gold. It is, as we see it, a matter for
Great Britain to decide without our interference
where the pound is to be stabilised in relation to
commodities and ultimately in relation to gold. This
view would not prevent us, perhaps, from agreeing,
on a temporary stabilisation of the two currencies*

as a help to other nations. But it would eliminate from the discussion a dangerous and useless argument about the ratio between the dollar and the pound.

We must avoid, it seems to me, an argument about the currencies similar to the argument about capital ships and cruisers and tanks at the Disarmament Conference. We can, and should, make separate decisions, and there is no need for a complicated negotiation on the subject. If we can remove this question from the realm of bargaining we can proceed further on the same principle. Our policy should be, I believe, to have concurrent and concerted domestic policies rather than to attempt immediate complicated international agreements. Both countries can, and should, make credit abundant and cheap with a view to forcing down long-term interest rates and stimulating capital investment. Both countries can adopt, and the United States has adopted, a programme of public works for the purpose of putting the new credit into use and of priming the economic machine. The United States, moreover, is organising control of agricultural and industrial production which has as its main purpose the prevention of further destructive cutting of prices and wages under the pressure of excess plant and excess labour. These, as I see it, are the main policies which the President is writing on the lovely blank sheets of writing paper with the beautifully sharp pencils that Congress has just provided him with. It is, I think, a fair interpretation of these policies to say that we regard measures for restoring purchasing power to farmers, miners and the unemployed as the greatest immediate contribution we can make to world recovery. Leaving out certain food crops we are normally, I believe, consumers of perhaps 40 per cent of the chief raw materials which enter into international trade. I do not know what the figures are for the British Empire, but they must be very large. So that a really bold concurrent attack upon the depression in Great Britain and America ought to have a decisive influence upon the whole world economy.

Such a course as I have been suggesting seems to me not only the most likely to be effective, but also to be the one way to avoid that long tedious fiasco which you described just a few minutes ago. It is a great advantage that it does not call for a complicated diplomatic negotiation; that it does not raise disturbing or wholly secondary questions of national advantage; that it is a course which the enlightened leaders of both countries would wish to pursue, even if there were no World Economic Conference. And yet it is a course which they can pursue far more effectively if they understand and sympathise with each other while they are pursuing it.

In the event that Great Britain and the United States, by concurrent policies, should try to lead the world out of the depression, we shall be fixing our hopes upon a policy which can be put into effect almost immediately. While these policies are being put into effect, the governments and the central banks can be preparing plans for improving world trade, for reviving international investment, for assisting the weaker nations and for reconstructing a world monetary standard. It is no use pretending, however, that these are not difficult and complicated matters, and the world cannot stand still while experts and statesmen and bankers argue about them. That is why the theory of a concurrent attack on the depression by the leading countries would seem to be the immediate need and also the most profitable subject for discussion at the London Conference. Don't you agree, Keynes?

KEYNES: Yes, Lippmann, I think that the general line of approach to the Conference's problems which you suggest is very likely the most helpful one. If an attempt is made to induce a large number of governments to enter into binding engagements on the spot, we can be quite sure that the wording will become so vague and ambiguous as to mean nothing. But I also see great risks of futility in mere declarations of agreement about the general lines of policy. For these can so easily result in no action whatever. After all, very sensible observations about the necessity of raising prices have been common form amongst governments for many months past. But nothing has been done about it.

You will lead me into such deep waters that some of our audience may drown if I try to follow up what you say about stabilising currencies separately on commodities. But this proposal is too vague as it stands. I am no friend of the gold standard, as you well know. But all the same, I think that gold can still provide a convenient link between English and American money, provided we agree that it is not to be a rigid link. I suggest that we should try to agree on four things. First of all, a fair parity between pounds and dollars on the basis of the existing situation. Next, that we fix approximately and for the time being only, the gold value of each on the basis of this parity. Third, that we hold ourselves free to alter by agreement the gold value of our currencies whilst keeping the relation between them the same. And finally, that each country should retain the right to ask for a change in the relation between the currencies if the future course of prices is different in the two countries. This last provision makes my proposal substantially the same as yours, but the general character of my plan is more definite.

The rest of your policy seems to me absolutely right–cheap money, public works, help for the farmers. If only the Conference could get even two or three of the major countries *committed* to these things, it would have laid the foundations for recovery. But I don't know that it will help much merely to announce that they are desirable.

Then you mustn't forget the desperate needs of the debtor countries. We shall hear much during the Conference of the unsupportable load of international debts and how it is impossible to wait for a problematical rise of prices to ease this burden.

There is, also, the important problem of tariffs. Must we not be ready to allow regional agreements for the reduction of tariffs between neighbours which do not apply universally? For this is the only kind of reduction which is practicable.

These things – and much more – are in the hands of the statesmen and their experts. What can our audience in the two countries do to help in the creation of that unheard, unspoken, but always palpable, force which governs the world–I mean public opinion? I think that the great public can play its part by allowing its feelings and its responses to the news to be governed by the simple virtues. Let us try not to be suspicious. Let us avoid the fear of being outdone in a close bargain. Let us seize every opening to approve positive solutions – not obstinate about our own particular plan if the plan of someone else seems also to end in the right direction.

In point of fact, where our interests are opposed to one another, the national advantage which is at stake will be on a trifling scale compared with what we should all gain if prosperity were to return. For prosperity would restore to us, many times over, the greatest possible sacrifice that any country could be asked to make. If we were creating all the wealth of which we are technically capable, we should have a vast margin in hand over any conceivable concessions. I know how difficult it is for a negotiator to live up to this when it comes down to details. But all the same, isn't this what they all ought to have at the back of their minds? And this, too, should be the governing thought of us members of the public who are outside the details. Public opinion, softly ebbing round the rock of the Conference like the waters of a surrounding ocean, should be consistently murmuring 'Amity, Agreement, Action'. We all of us are greedy, competitive, obstinate and suspicious in international affairs, unless we are on our guard. And, above all, let not public opinion lag behind the delegates in its sensitiveness. When delegates meet face to face and find that the other man is a reasonable human being, friendliness and a spirit of accommodation soon spring up. And then, sometimes, public opinion, knowing nothing but the cold and hostile abstraction of an alien country, damps down these kindly feelings. I plead, therefore, for an atmosphere of compromise and reasonableness. I do not ask for signatures to binding agreements; but I do ask for genuine decisions, which those making them intend to carry out, designed to raise prices and restore employment by increasing the effective purchasing power of all the peoples of the world. For there is no other means whatever of accomplishing our purpose. And this, fortunately, is one of the cases where the success of one country will help all the others to success. I trust you feel as I do, Lippmann.

LIPPMANN: *Well, Keynes, we haven't much time left. So let me say in one sentence that I am in entire agreement with you about the spirit in which statesmen and peoples ought to approach this Conference. In the specific question of the currencies I should go along with you on the desirability of seeing whether we can make such a tentative agreement as you have outlined. What I do think is most important, however, is that our two countries should not become deadlocked in a negotiation about the parity between the dollar and the pound. If they do, I greatly fear that attention will be distracted from the much more promising business of getting two or three of the largest countries committed to a policy of cheap money, public works, and the restoration of purchasing power.*

Finally, speaking as an American, I should not be candid if I failed to mention the payment of War debts due on 15 June. My own view has always been that to the American people these debts were not worth the financial dislocation and the political disturbance which they produce. The majority of my countrymen do not take this view, and therefore, it is, I imagine, impossible to hope for a final settlement of this troublesome question within the next few days. But, if a final settlement cannot be arranged, it seems to me imperative that the Governments of Great Britain and the United States should find some way of postponing the issue–that, in other words, there should be neither insistence on payment nor insistence on default. The two Governments simply must find a way to avoid insistence either on payment or on default. If they cannot arrange so simple a matter as that, what right have their statesmen to talk about peace and reconstruction in the world?

Roosevelt's Economic Experiments

[13 January 1934][1]

Keynes had watched the development of New Deal policies from afar in 1933, reserving his comments to the currency policies which had taken the United States off the gold standard. Until the autumn, when the Administration began to intervene in the market to raise the dollar price of gold, the U.S. dollar had floated against those currencies which had remained tied to gold or those currencies whose authorities did not intervene in the markets to influence the course of their exchange rate with the dollar. However, the Administration had refused to enter an exchange-rate stabilisation agreement with Britain and France for the duration of the World Economic Conference and President Roosevelt's 'bombshell' message rejecting a draft declaration on exchange stabilisation, released on

---

[1] *The Listener,* 17 January, 1934; XXI, 305–9.

3 July, effectively ended the Conference. Keynes had been a party to the American side of the pre-bombshell discussion in London in late June and early July.

After the Conference, Keynes's interest broadened to the whole range of New Deal policies, but it was not until the end of the year that he found the ideal means of discussing them – an open letter. The idea seems to have come from Felix Frankfurter, the American lawyer and legal philosopher whom Keynes had known since they worked together in Paris in 1919, who was spending the 1933–4 academic year as a visiting professor at Oxford. Frankfurter was Keynes's guest for the Founder's Feast at King's on 6 December 1933 and the two of them talked about a possible letter. By 15 December, Keynes had more or less completed the letter. He passed it on to Frankfurter who would get it to the President before it appeared in the *New York Times* on 31 December.[2]

In January, Keynes continued his discussion with a broadcast.

The economic experiments of President Roosevelt may prove, I think, to be of extraordinary importance in economic history, because, for the first time – at least I cannot recall a comparable case – theoretical advice is being taken by one of the rulers of the world as the basis of large-scale action. The possibility of such a remarkable event has arisen out of the utter and

---

[2] XXI, 289–97.

complete discredit of every variety of orthodox advice. The state of mind in America which lies behind this willingness to try unorthodox experiments arises out of an economic situation desperate beyond precedent.

Although we here feel ourselves to have suffered a pretty severe slump, it is, all the same, hard for us to conceive the pass that things had reached in America a year ago. Unemployment nearly twice as bad as the worst we ever had; the farmers ruined; the banks insolvent; no hope apparent in any direction; and all this only three years after such a pinnacle of pride and prosperity as no other country in the world had ever reached. Moreover, the culminating point of these economic disasters had been reached after a period during which orthodox financial advice and high financial circles of the United States were believed to be exerting great influence over President Hoover and his advisers. This, then, seemed to be the result of following so-called sound opinion. Then, on top of this, came the financial scandals, which were taken by the general public to discredit the financial leaders morally as much as the ruinous state of affairs had appeared to discredit them intellectually.

It is impossible to appreciate what is now happening in the United States unless one realises this background for the so-called New Deal, with orthodox advice contemptuously rejected and the head of the government turning right away from the financiers and all the so-called practical men to theorists and idealists with little or no experience of affairs.

It is not surprising that some confusion should result. The President himself is not, and does not pretend to be, an economist. Economics, one must confess, is at the moment a backward science, whatever one's hopes are for the future, in which semi-obsolete ideas are widely influential, hardly less in academic circles than elsewhere. It must have been difficult for the President to know in what direction to turn for the best available advice. In practice he has shown himself extraordinarily accessible to anyone with new ideas to air whom he believed to be independent and disinterested. Naturally he had received a great deal of advice, some of it inconsistent with the rest and not all of it of equal quality. Himself an empiricist, not wedded to any particular doctrine or any one technique, tolerant, optimistic, courageous and patient, he has been happy to provide the political skill and the power of authority to give some sort of a run to all kinds of *ideas,* ready to judge by results, but admittedly experimenting and watching carefully to drop in time schemes, the actual operation of which began to seem dangerous or disappointing.

Thus, the President himself has been content with general notions, a conduit pipe for the more general ideas of others, considering quite rightly that detail is not his business. He has not been solely concerned with lifting the United States out of its disastrous slump. He is just as much interested, perhaps even more, in many liberal reforms, some of them long overdue. Above all, he has been deliberately standing for the small man, the employee, the small investor, the small farmer, the bank depositor, the owner of small savings, against high finance and big business. Everyone has felt that this was his general position. That without doubt is the main explanation of the extraordinary popularity which has made him for the moment as powerful a dictator in the United States as any of the other less constitutional dictators of the contemporary world.

It would be a big job even to run through the headings of the measures already taken to carry the New Deal into law. I can only mention one or two. The National Industrial Recovery Act, or N.R.A., includes such social legislation as, for example, the abolition of child labour and the regulation of hours. It also tries to provide for organised planning, industry by industry, whilst avoiding the abuses of the trust or the cartel. Apart from this Act there are the measures to help the farmers – provisions for the reduction of their mortgage interest, funds to buy up and hold surplus crops, and inducements to restrict crops where there has been overproduction. Then there are the President's financial measures to enable depositors in insolvent banks to get their money back and to guarantee them against similar losses in future. Help, too, for small investors through the Securities Act, which is largely based on our own legislation for the protection of investors, though in some respects it goes beyond our own Acts.

Most important of all in the short run, and also most dubious and controversial, are the President's monetary measures; partly designed to help the debtor class by raising prices, and partly aimed at curing unemployment. One half of this programme has consisted in abandoning the gold standard, which was probably wise, and in taking various measures – very technical, but, in my opinion, not very useful – to depreciate the gold value of the dollar below its natural level. It is important that monetary arrangements should not hamper business expansion, but it is not easy to bring about business expansion *merely* by monetary manipulation. The other half of his programme, however, is infinitely more important and offers in my opinion much greater hopes. I mean the attempt to cure unemployment by large-scale expenditure on public works and similar purposes. This part of his programme has been very slow to get moving. As recently as the end of October practically nothing had been spent, and as a result of this, employment and output were again falling away. But recently the expenditure seems to have been more substantial. The President's recent sensational budget statement which was in the papers a fortnight ago means vast expenditure on these heads in the near future – if he is able to live up to his programme. Public works, railway renewals, unemployment relief, subsidies to local authorities, further aid to farmers and so forth make up the enormous so-called deficit – much of which, however, will be covered by valuable assets. I doubt whether it will prove practicable for his Administration to live up to their full programme. It may take more time to put it into effect than is now intended. But, if the President succeeds in carrying out a substantial part of his programme, for my part I expect a great

improvement in American industry and employment within six months.

At any rate those of us – and we are many – who
hate the idea of revolution and the uprooting of all
those good things which grow slowly, yet are discon-
certed at our present failure to seize our opportunity
to solve the problem of poverty, will hope to the bottom of our hearts that a man who is thus trying new
ways boldly and even gaily with no object but the
welfare of his people will manage to succeed.

I believe he will win the first round. The testing
time, the more difficult task, will come afterwards –
to hold the gains once made and to avoid the fatal
relapses which in recent times have always charac-
terised our economic system.

Keynes soon had an opportunity for an American
visit. Columbia University had offered him an hon-
orary degree. Working around 5 June, the date of
the Columbia Convocation, he managed to spend
three weeks in New York and Washington, where he
had an hour with President Roosevelt on 28 May.
The BBC attempted to arrange a broadcast of Keynes's
reactions to America. The original plan was to broadcast from the *RMS Olympic* as he returned home, but
the ship did not have the necessary equipment and
by the time Keynes was in London he was too busy
making up five weeks of arrears to find the time.[3]

---

[3] CKKP, BR/3, JMK to C. Siepmann, 18 June 1934.

Is the Economic System Self-Adjusting?

[19 November 1934][1]

In the fall of 1934 Keynes took part in a broadcast series of 12 talks under the rubric 'Poverty in Plenty'. In his talk, which came towards the end of the series, Keynes referred to the talks of most of the other participants or to the syllabuses that they had prepared for participants in various BBC discussion groups. I list the titles of the papers in the order in which Keynes referred to them. All of these were reprinted in *The Burden of Plenty?* (ed. Graham Hutton) which appeared from Allen and Unwin in 1935.

H.D. Henderson, *The Slump and the Growth of Productive Power*

R.H. Brand, *A Banker's View of the Problem*

---

[1] *The Listener,* 21 November 1934; XIII, 485–92.

Lionel Robbins, *The Two-fold Roots of the Great
    Depression: Inflation and Intervention*
Hugh Dalton, *Our Present Discontents*
J.A. Hobson, *Under-Consumption and its Remedies*
A.R. Orage, *Social Credit*
Barbara Wootton, *The Necessity of Planning*

If we consider what has been said in these talks so
far, it is clear, I think, that there is one point about
which we all agree – a point which was rightly
emphasised by Mr Henderson. The point is this.
Whatever may be the best remedy for poverty in
plenty, we must reject all those alleged remedies
which consist, in substance, of getting rid of the
plenty. It may be true, for various reasons, that, as
the potential plenty increases, the problem of getting the fruits of it distributed to the great body of
consumers will present increasing difficulties. But it
is to the analysis and solution of these difficulties
that we must direct our minds. To seek an escape by
making the productive machine less productive
must be wrong. I often find myself in favour of
measures to restrict output as a temporary palliative
or to meet an emergency. But the temper of mind
which turns too easily to restriction is dangerous.
For it has nothing useful to contribute to the permanent solution.

But this is another way of saying that we must not
regard the conditions of supply – that is to say, our
facilities to produce – as being the fundamental
source of our troubles. And, if this is agreed, it seems

to follow that it is the conditions of demand which our diagnosis must search and probe for the explanation. Indeed, it is, I think, fair to say that all the contributors to these talks meet to this extent on common ground. If you will examine carefully what they have told you will find that each one of them finds the major part of his explanation in some factor which relates to the conditions of demand. But though we, your mentors, all start out in the same direction, we soon part company into two main groups. And even within each group every one of us has a somewhat different explanation of what is wrong with demand, and, consequently, a different idea of the right remedy. Between us, perhaps, we shall succeed in giving you a fair sample of the competing opinions of the contemporary world.

I have said that we fall into two main groups. What makes the cleavage which thus divides us? On the one side are those who believe that the existing economic system is, in the long run, a self-adjusting system, though with creaks and groans and jerks, and interrupted by time lags, outside interference and mistakes. Of those who adhere, broadly speaking, to this school of thought, Mr Henderson lays stress on the increased difficulty of *rapid* self-adjustment to change, rightly attaching importance to the greater loss and delay involved in a change-over from one type of production to another – when changes in technique or in tastes make this necessary – in an environment where population and markets are no longer expanding rapidly; Mr Brand stresses the growing tendency for outside interference to hinder the processes of self-adjustment; and Professor Robbins, to judge from his syllabus, stresses the effect of business mistakes under the influence of the uncertainty and the false expectations due to the faults of post-war monetary systems. These authorities do not, of course, believe that the system is automatically or immediately self-adjusting. But they do believe that it has an inherent tendency towards self-adjustment, if it is not interfered with and if the action of change and chance is not too rapid.

On the other side of the gulf are those who reject the idea that the existing economic system is, in any significant sense, self-adjusting. They believe that the failure of effective demand to reach the full potentialities of supply, in spite of human psychological demand being immensely far from satisfied for the vast majority of individuals, is due to much more fundamental causes. Dr Dalton stresses the great inequality of incomes which causes a separation between the power to consume and the desire to consume. Mr Hobson believes that the great resources at the disposal of the entrepreneur are a chronic cause of his setting up plant capable of producing more than the limited resources of the consumer can absorb. Mr Orage demanded a method of increasing consumer power to overcome the difficulties pointed out by Dr Dalton and Mr Hobson. Mrs Wootton, who is to contribute to this series next week, calls for planning, although she only half-rejects the theory of self-adjustment, having not yet reached, one feels, a synthesis satisfactory to herself between her intellectual theory and her spiritual home.

The gulf between these two schools of thought is deeper, I believe, than most of those on either side of it are aware of. On which side does the essential truth lie? That is the vital question for us to solve. That is the overshadowing problem of which these talks should make you clearly conscious, if they are to serve their purpose.

I can scarcely begin here to give you the reasons for what I believe to be the right answer. But I can tell you on which side of the gulf I myself stand; and I can give you a brief indication of what has to be settled before either school can thoroughly dispose of its adversary.

The strength of the self-adjusting school depends on its having behind it almost the whole body of organised economic thinking and doctrine of the past hundred years. This is a formidable power. It is the product of acute minds and has persuaded and convinced the great majority of the intelligent and disinterested persons who have studied it. It has vast prestige and a more far-reaching influence than is obvious. For it lies behind the education and the habitual modes of thought, not only of economists but also of bankers and business men and civil servants and politicians of all parties. The essential elements in it are fervently accepted by Marxists. Indeed, Marxism is a highly plausible inference from the Ricardian economics, that capitalistic individualism cannot possibly work in practice. So much so, that, if Ricardian economics were to fall, an essential prop to the intellectual foundations of Marxism would fall with it.

Thus, if the heretics on the other side of the gulf are to demolish the forces of nineteenth-century orthodoxy – and I include Marxism in orthodoxy equally with *laissez-faire*, these two being the nineteenth-century twins of Say and Ricardo – they must attack them in their citadel. No successful attack has yet been made. The heretics of today are the descendants of a long line of heretics who, overwhelmed but never extinguished, have survived as isolated groups of cranks. They are deeply dissatisfied. They believe that common observation is enough to show that facts do not conform to the orthodox reasoning. They propose remedies prompted by instinct, by flair, by practical good sense, by experience of the world – half-right, most of them, and half-wrong. Contemporary discontents have given them a volume of popular support and an opportunity for propagating their ideas such as they have not had for several generations. But they have made no impression on the citadel. Indeed, many of them accept the orthodox premises themselves; and it is only because their, flair is stronger than their logic that they do not accept its conclusions.

Now *I* range myself with the heretics. I believe their flair and their instinct move them towards the right conclusion. But I was brought up in the citadel and I recognise its power and might. A large part of the established body of economic doctrine I cannot but accept as broadly correct. I do not doubt it. For me, therefore, it is impossible to rest satisfied until I can put my finger on the flaw in that part of the orthodox reasoning which leads to the conclusions which for various reasons seem to me to be inacceptable. I believe that I am on my way to do so. There is, I am convinced, a fatal flaw in that part of the orthodox reasoning which deals with the theory of what determines the level of effective demand and the volume of aggregate employment; the flaw being largely due to the failure of the classical doctrine to develop a satisfactory theory of the rate of interest.

Put very briefly, the point is something like this. Any individual, if he finds himself with a certain income, will, according to his habits, his tastes and his motives towards prudence, spend a portion of it on consumption and the rest he will save. If his income increases, he will almost certainly consume more than before but it is highly probable that he will also save more. That is to say, he will not increase his consumption by the full amount of the increase in his income. Thus if a given national income is less equally divided, or, if the national income increases so that individual incomes are greater than before, the gap between total incomes and the total expenditure on consumption is likely to widen. But incomes can only be generated by producing goods for consumption or by producing goods for use as capital. Thus the gap between total incomes and expenditure on consumption *cannot* be greater than the amount of new capital which it is thought worthwhile to produce. Consequently, our habit of withholding from consumption an increasing sum as our incomes increase means that it is impossible for our incomes to increase unless either we change our habits to consume more or the business world calculates that it is worthwhile to produce more capital goods. For, failing both these alternatives, the increased employment and output, by which alone increased incomes can be generated, will prove unprofitable and will not persist.

Now the school which believes in self-adjustment is, in fact, assuming that the rate of interest adjusts itself more or less automatically, to encourage just the right amount of production of capital goods to keep our incomes at the maximum level which our energies and our organisation and our knowledge of how to produce efficiently are capable of providing. This is, however, pure assumption. There is no theoretical reason for believing it to be true. A very moderate amount of observation of the facts, unclouded by preconceptions, is sufficient to show that they do not bear it out. Those standing on my side of the gulf, whom I have ventured to describe as half-right and half-wrong, have perceived this; and they conclude that the only remedy is for us to change the distribution of wealth and modify our habits in such a way as to increase our propensity to spend our incomes on current consumption. I agree with them in thinking that this would be a remedy. But I disagree with them when they go further and argue that it is the only remedy. For there is an alternative, namely, to increase the output of capital goods by reducing the rate of interest and in other ways.

When the rate of interest has fallen to a very low figure and has remained there sufficiently long to show that there is no further capital construction worth doing even at that low rate, then I should agree that the facts point to the necessity of drastic social changes directed towards increasing consumption. For it would be clear that we already had as great a stock of capital as we could usefully employ.

Even as things are, there is a strong presumption that a greater equality of incomes would lead to increased employment and greater aggregate income. But hitherto the rate of interest has been too high to allow us to have all the capital goods, particularly houses, which would be useful to us. Thus, at present, it is important to maintain a careful balance between stimulating consumption and stimulating investment. Economic welfare and social well-being will be increased in the long run by a policy which tends to make capital goods so abundant, that the reward which can be gained from owning them falls to so modest a figure as to be no longer a serious burden on anyone. The right course is to get rid of the scarcity of capital goods – which will rid us at the same time of most of the evils of capitalism – whilst also moving in the direction of increasing the share of income falling to those whose economic welfare will gain most by their having the chance to consume more.

None of this, however, will happen by itself or of its own accord. The system is not self-adjusting, and, without purposive direction, it is incapable of translating our actual poverty into our potential plenty.

To develop so fundamental a matter any further than this would obviously lead us far beyond the opportunities of this brief talk. I will add no more than this: if the basic system of thought on which Mr Henderson, Mr Brand and Professor Robbins rely is, in its essentials, unassailable, then there is no escape from their broad conclusions, namely, that whilst there are increasingly perplexing problems and plenty of opportunities to make disastrous mistakes, yet nevertheless we must keep our heads and depend on the ultimate soundness of the traditional teaching – the proposals of the heretics, however plausible and even advantageous in the short run, being essentially superficial and ultimately dangerous. Only if they are successfully attacked in the citadel can we reasonably ask them to look at the problem in a radically new way.

Meanwhile I hope we shall await, with what patience we can command, a successful outcome of the great activity of thought amongst economists today – a fever of activity such as has not been known for a century. We are, in my very confident belief – a belief, I fear, shared by few, either on the right or on the left – at one of those uncommon junctures of human affairs where we can be saved by the solution of an intellectual problem, and in no other way. If we know the whole truth already, we shall not succeed indefinitely in avoiding a clash of human passions seeking an escape from the intolerable. But I have a better hope.

Meanwhile, it is not unlikely that English principles of compromise will mitigate the evils of the situation by leading statesmen and administrators to temper the worst consequences of the errors of the teaching in which they have been brought up by doing things which are quite inconsistent with their own principles, in practice neither orthodox nor heretic, of which some signs are already manifest.

IV

Education and the Arts

The following broadcasts bring together another strand of Keynes's commentaries as a public intellectual. There is only one published paper on education – the broadcast printed below. Most of his writings on the arts, which have been collected together in the *Collected Writings* (XXVIII, ch. 4), consisted of unsigned puffs and short comments for the columns of the *Nation and Athenaeum*, reviews for the *Nation* and the *New Statesman*, prefaces to exhibition catalogues, letters to the press and a few longer discussions.

University Men in Business

[16 February 1927][1]

This 1927 discussion with the industrialist Ernest Walls was chaired by Sir Ernest Benn a noted publisher and publicist.

SIR ERNEST BENN: *We are going to have a conversation or discussion – I am not at all clear how it ought to be described – on the question of 'University Men in Business'. We are to have the advantage of hearing Mr Maynard Keynes and Mr Ernest Walls, and it is my function to stand, or sit, between these two experts and, as chairman, keep them in order.*

Mr Walls as the Managing Director of Lever Bros Ltd will speak with very exceptional authority on the subject from the point of view of the business man. No one can tell us better than he can what it is that business looks to secure from the universities. On the other hand, we are fortunate in being able to hear Mr J. M. Keynes on the other side of

---

[1] XIX, 649–61.

the question; and he will be able to tell us how the universities look at the matter, and what it is that the universities can give to the business life of the nation.

There are all sorts of great big questions involved in this discussion. First, the difference between education and instruction. Is a university education the basis upon which a business career can be subsequently built and to which business knowledge can be added, or is it suggested that the universities can actually teach a man how to do business? But there are bigger and more immediate questions. There is the vital matter of industrial peace, a matter which is exercising the minds of every serious citizen today. Surely no one will deny that industrial peace would be easier of achievement if both branches of the industrial army possessed a higher degree of education?

I notice in a recent discussion on this same question a reference to the class instinct of the undergraduate. Class instinct is surely a bad thing, and I hope that Mr Keynes will be able to show us that the universities are able to break down, and not in fact to build up, anything in the nature of class instinct. As a business man without a university education, I have always suspected a certain snobbery developed by the universities which drives most of their products into professions – the civil service, the arts and other sidelines in human endeavour. Surely the main line of human endeavour must always be the production of the material requirements of the human race, and that is business.

As I hope Mr Keynes may be able to tell us that the universities are looking more and more to business as a profession and as a career, so I hope Mr Walls will be able to assure us that business men are looking more and more to the universities to supply the recruits for the business of the future.

My job, however, is not to carry on this discussion – merely to introduce. My instructions from Mr Sieveking were to introduce for five minutes. Having to the best of my ability complied with that command, I am now going to ask you to listen to Mr Walls.

MR WALLS: *In your kind introduction, Sir Ernest, you said that my function would be to state as far as I can what appeared to be the requirements of business – what business calls for from the universities. I fear it is a little difficult, apart from the immensity of the subject, because I am myself prejudiced, as I am bound to say at the outset, in favour of the university man in business, as my own career has been that I entered business immediately. I came down from the university and have remained in the same business ever since. As far as I am personally concerned, any success I have had in business I put down entirely to my university training.*

CHAIRMAN: *Entirely?*

WALLS: *Yes, I think so. I think I would say entirely. Where I think the universities can help us in business especially is in the direction making the career of business more of a profession than it is today. You said just now that the universities are turning out men for certain professions such as the church, the civil service, the law and so on. Apparently today it is expected that an undergraduate at the end of his career will leap straight from the university into business and settle down immediately into it. No one expects the same thing of a lawyer or any other professional man; and I think that this gap between the professional life of business and the previous training is the greatest difficulty that we have to face, and – to be perfectly frank – the universities do not, as it seems to me, make any real effort to fill that gap.*

My point about the professional character of business, I think, is well reinforced by the experience of the present time when more and more important positions in business are being occupied by professional men – lawyers, for instance, are becoming more and more business men – and this I take to be on account of their professional training. The present day business world is largely made up of limited liability companies in which the directors are in effect trustees for shareholders. Then again business is being done on a very much larger scale than has ever been the case and, in addition, we have in every direction amalgamations and combines which are not only national but also are tending to become international, so that the men who will be required to direct and organise these modern types of business must be professional in the sense that they have been definitely trained for the position they will occupy and have had the advantage of the highest education which we can give them. In

*a word, what modern business calls for is a profes-
sionally trained business man and the question is:
Can the universities provide him in the same way
that they have successfully supplied the older professions?*

CHAIRMAN: *What do you say to that, Mr Keynes?*

MR MAYNARD KEYNES: The men whom the universities have supplied to the business world in the
past have belonged to two quite distinct types.
There are, first of all, the sons of wealthy business parents who are sent to a public school and
a university with the idea from the outset that
they will, at the end of it all, find a safe berth
in the family business or in some other concern
where the family has influence. This will work
out according to programme, unless the young
man shows himself quite unusually incompe-
tent. He has no great incentive to stretch his
energies in any direction which is not naturally
agreeable to him. The degree he takes will not
be too much scrutinised. For him, the university is a pleasant and delightful interlude without much serious bearing on his future career.

The other type consists of undergraduates
with no family or other influence in the business world, who are faced with the necessity of
earning a living immediately after the conclusion of their university career, and have nothing
but themselves to depend upon. These young
men are naturally, as a rule, pretty serious
workers. They measure themselves against

their contemporaries; and those who know them through their three university years can probably form a shrewd judgement at the end of that time, both about their brains and about their temperamental suitability for one walk of life or another.

Now, in the past, the majority of university men in business have belonged as a rule to the first type. I hold no brief for these. I hope the university does them no harm: I think it may do some of them quite a lot of good. But it is not for what they have learned at their university that they have been selected for a business career, and I don't think that it's the universities who should be blamed, if parental affection had encouraged them to lead too easy a life when they were young and has put them in too safe a job when they were grown up. Indeed, my own opinion is that hereditary influence in higher business appointments is one of the greatest dangers to efficiency in British business. So many of our industries are now reaching a difficult age. They are becoming second- and third- generation businesses. They are getting into the hands of men who didn't create them and who couldn't possibly have created them.

I fancy, however, that the other type, those who have been deliberately chosen on the ground of their university record, is going to become increasingly important. There has always been a certain number of this type entering business, but it is a comparatively new thing for them to do so in large numbers. In the case of the University of Cambridge (about which I know most), it dates from the development of the University Appointments Board, which is an organisation, the whole purpose of which is to keep in touch with the requirements of the business world and to make sure that no one is recommended from Cambridge who isn't well suited to the job offered, not only by his intellectual attainments but also by character and temperament. A man's university career ought to be a testing time. Universities can reasonably claim to be judged by the success of those who are selected because they have passed successfully through this testing time, and not by those who have passed straight on through family influence, quite irrespective of what they may have done at the university or what their university thinks of them.

CHAIRMAN: *Have you in mind any examples of men who have been selected on the sole ground of their university success?*

KEYNES: Well, Sir Ernest, there is one very big concern – the Shell Oil Group, which has now been taking men from Cambridge regularly through the Appointments Board for some twenty years, so that they have now had time to estimate the success of this method from pretty long experience. Sir Robert Waley Cohen, Director of the Shell Group (who, by the way, is a good specimen himself of the university man in business), in speaking to his shareholders recently after a visit to the East, told them that the thing which stood out and impressed itself on him more than anything else was the remarkable staff by which the Company was served. 'Many of them,' he said, 'joined us originally straight from the university, and they constitute today a highly trained and intelligent body of men who are serving our interests with devotion and ability. There is more active competition in the oil business today than at any time within my memory. But we are holding our own, and I think we owe this, as much as to any other single factor, to a unique staff.' The Secretary of one of the Argentine Railways, who has been taking Cambridge men lately, reports that the only difficulty the Company has is that other people are so anxious to snap their men up. I know another great company trading in India and the East which is now almost exclusively staffed by men of good academic attainments, mostly from a single Cambridge College, judging by results certainly one of the most prosperous concerns in the country.

CHAIRMAN: *Well, Mr Walls, what have you to say to that?*

WALLS: *Those are very useful examples, Mr Keynes. What I would be interested to know is what kind of vocational training, if any, followed the university course in these cases.*

It seems to me that there is probably required for business something in the nature of such vocational training (either immediately following the university career or overlapping with it), in the same way that the lawyer has a specialised legal education, for example; and this is a point on which I am sure Mr Keynes you can give us some very useful suggestions, for I feel strongly that it is here that the real gap exists. Of course, for highly specialised work – engineering, chemistry and so on – vocational training of university type exists, and I imagine it is realised by everybody that for such careers it is absolutely essential; but I am thinking more of the commercial side of business rather than any specialised part and, indeed, more of what we might call commerce than what would be classed as production.

Then, there is the international side of business and the utter lack of foreign languages amongst our business people. We have gone on for several generations in our insular pride without finding it necessary to learn any other language than our own. This is hardly likely to continue to be possible, all the more so if one of the features of the immediate future is the internationalisation of business, which will certainly bring great demands in the direction of language.

KEYNES: My own view, Mr Walls, is that it is a mistake for the universities to attempt vocational training. Their business is to develop a man's intelligence and character in such a way that he can pick up relatively quickly the special details of that business he turns to subsequently. I am sure that the special training you speak of is something that can only be taught by business men to business men. I agree with you about languages; and there, I think, the universities are open to criticism and, perhaps, the schools even more. Every young man ought to have mastered either French or German (preferably both) by spending some of his vacations abroad, by the time he leaves the university.

CHAIRMAN: *In that case it will be vacational and not vocational training? Where, then, would you draw the line? Does chemistry come within the category of vocational training? What about engineering, electrical engineering? Where do you stop?*

KEYNES: I doubt if any of these things come into the scheme that Mr Walls mentioned. The engineering laboratory at Cambridge, which trains a great number of men for business, is a totally different thing from actual engineering works. The chemistry we teach is a necessary foundation for the commercial chemist, but, fortunately for its educational value, it is in itself something totally different from the work of the average, commercial chemist.

WALLS: *I think the greatest complaint which I have come across myself amongst businessmen when they are talking about this question of university men and the alleged failure of university men to make good in business, their greatest objection, is that the university man when he comes down and enters into business is apt to take a theoretical view about the various questions and problems that come before him.*

KEYNES*:* What do you mean by 'theoretical'?

WALLS: What do I mean by 'theoretical'? I think the businessman calls theoretical any effort to deal with a problem in a general way rather than bringing it down to what he would call 'Brass tacks'.

KEYNES: May not a training, when they are young to look at the world rather more broadly, help them to take a more profound view of things when they have added business experience to their education?

WALLS: *The difficulty is this. A young man of 23, say, entering a business without any knowledge of that business, is immediately pitted against other young men of the same age who have had a good many years in the business and know all manner of practical details connected with the business – facts and figures and so on, of which he is obviously completely ignorant. It is one of the difficulties, I think. A university man will get the essential facts and figures in a very short time, but in the early stages he is likely to be subject to criticism. Possibly the answer is in an intermediate period of vocational training for business following the university – I agree with you, Mr Keynes, that it is not the university's function to give this training and that it must be linked up with actual business. But there is, I think, undoubtedly amongst businessmen a feeling that the university man is rather apt to look on the practical questions with too airy a view, his head rather in the skies. That may possibly be a self-protective device of the businessman.*

One last point is this. I feel strongly myself that we want university men in business, properly trained and ready for business, because business itself is in such desperate need. When we have over a million unemployed as a regular feature of our national life it cannot be said that the businessmen of the country, whatever their difficulties, have really succeeded in paying a national dividend. And many of our existing business methods need considerable reinforcement at the present time if we are to compete successfully with America, for example. There seems a need of new points of view, and it is to the young men who have had the advantage of the finest education and training that we know how to give them that we ought to be looking for the reconstruction of British business.

KEYNES: What we do want in this country is some general scheme of training worked out by the big businesses themselves. I believe that large engineering concerns, like Daimlers and Metropolitan-Vickers, already have an elaborate and well thought-out scheme for training their university apprentices. I rather think that Sir Hugo Hurst of the General Electric Company was the first man in this country to set up a regular

training scheme in the business for producing
commercial material from the universities. I believe that is the right line, rather than to try to
drive university teachers to attempt something
for which they have no real qualifications.

CHAIRMAN: *I remember one of the first Mayors of the
London Boroughs who on election said that he
hoped to discharge the duties of the h'office without partiality on the one 'and or h'impartiality on
the h'other. That was twenty-five years ago, but
it's a statement of the principles of good chair-
manship which I have never failed to remember.
As Chairman, I can agree with both of these distinguished debaters, or I can discharge my duties
equally satisfactorily by differing from both of
them. And in a way I do differ, at all events on
some points from what has been said by Mr Keynes
and Mr Walls.*

*It seems to me that we ought to have started by
defining business. We have talked about industry:
we have talked technicalities. But we don't seem
to have on the table, as it were, a very clearly
defined notion as to what business is. The world at
the moment is full of producers who know how to
produce, who want to produce their own products,
and who don't seem to me at least, to pay much
attention to what the consumer wants. I would
define business as bringing the producer and consumer together – to me the most difficult function
in the whole of the work of providing us with the
necessities of life.*

But that by the way. I want for the moment to do a little quarrelling with each of my friends.

Don't you think, Mr Keynes, that you are a little bit hard on what may be described as the hereditary business, though it is, of course, true that there are cases where pampered sons are jobbed into father's business, and this goes on.

KEYNES: I am not referring to the extreme cases. They drop out soon enough.

CHAIRMAN: *But have you made enough allowance for the fact that some businesses at least are really more than one life's work? For instance, in my business of publishing and journalism, it is now commonly supposed that you must have enough printers' ink in the blood to succeed in it. I feel that there is a great deal in that. One life is often too short a time to know all there is to know about the intricacies and complexities of many of our trades. Only a few weeks ago, I heard a Scotchman make a twenty minutes' speech on the herring, from the boyhood of his grandfather to the evening of his own life devoted to the study of the herring, and at the end he calculated that he was just beginning to understand something about that useful and modest commodity. You can name concerns where the family tradition is the basis of the business.*

Now, turning to Mr Walls, I am going to quarrel even more definitely with him.

He said his success was entirely due to his university training – a most serious statement for one of our princes of commerce to make: I ventured to interrupt him and make him repeat the word 'entirely'. I know nothing of his business except as an observer and admirer. He is associated in my mind with two great big things – good soap and good advertising – and I should like to hear from him what the University of Oxford did in giving him a training in either.

KEYNES: I am surprised that you do not consider Oxford a good training for advertising.

WALLS: *Answering your point, Sir Ernest, we need in all industry efficient production of goods and efficient marketing of goods. That I think is what you mean by 'good soap and good advertising'. Now as regards production with which the technical side of business is mainly concerned I think it would be universally agreed that we require in our managements the highest scientific skill attainable – the highest standards of scientific education and training.*

CHAIRMAN: *But this is that point I made as to defining the nature of business. I should say that your technical man really belongs to a higher grade of labour. He is concerned with production; he may be concerned with the industry, but not with business.*

WALLS: *I agree, I agree. And I endeavoured in my remarks to differentiate between production and business or if you like the commercial side of business: the two things are distinct.*

Then, of course, you come to the advertising side, if you regard that as commerce.

CHAIRMAN: *I regard that as the essence of the commercial side of business.*

WALLS: *Well then if we are to take advertising and sell-*
ing as the essence of business and in an age where
production is always overtaking demand they are
certainly of prime importance, is it not in this field
especially that you want a clear mind, a man with
his brains trained to think, to generalise and analyse
situations, perhaps more than in any other branch
of business? What businessmen are apt to think is
that the marketing of goods is a spectacular corner
of business; that if you are a born showman, if I
may use that term, you will be able to sell anything.
My own view about the selling problem of business
is that, first of all, it is an analytical question and
that the whole subject can be made, and in many
directions is being made, a very scientific job indeed;
but if it is, then you want men who have had a con-
siderable training in the art of analysis and of clear
thinking. Apart from that you want something else,
which is the biggest need we have in business. You
want the creative ability. Everybody is born with a
creative instinct, and that instinct can be developed
in many ways, but the finest way of developing it so
as to bring the best results is by suitable education.
This need of creative ability I would count our great-
est need in business today; and while, of course,
there will always be geniuses arising who possess
that ability inborn to an extraordinary degree, it
is perfectly certain that in some measure it is an
inborn faculty and can be to a considerable extent
trained and developed successfully, and to a much
greater extent than at present. Creative ability and

imagination – these are the great needs of the busi-
ness of the future: Can we look to the universities to
supply them in the businessmen of the future?

CHAIRMAN: *Well, Mr Keynes, it seems to me that I shall*
have to appeal to you from the Chair, even if you do
come from Cambridge, to put in a word for advertis-
ing and salesmanship. Mr Walls's modesty seems
to need correcting. Surely, if you look to America,
where business and industry have succeeded in a
way unknown in any other country and at any
other time, advertising has developed to an extent
which we don't begin to understand here.

KEYNES: Well, Sir Ernest, advertising has become
a highly intellectual business. That is a reason
why the universities may be useful in regard
to it. But I think Mr Walls put his finger on
the practical difficulty when he dwelt on the
problem confronting the university man immediately on his leaving the university and arriv-
ing at his business appointment. Obviously he
will be extremely 'green' at first. He will naturally be an object of some amusement.

CHAIRMAN: *Yes I agree.*

KEYNES: Half the trouble would disappear if businessmen would pay him, in spite of that, a
reasonable salary from the beginning (having
regard to the expense of his education), and
find some way of training him for the higher
work of the business. For example, if the managing director can give such a man a post as his
private secretary and let him see from the inside

all his own problems and all the matters that arise in running a big business. Experience of a year or two of that kind will probably do more to make him fit to take his place than years in other departments.

WALLS: *I would rather see him starting with all his training, at the bottom of the ladder. Of course he is going to mount it much faster than the untrained man ever could do.*

KEYNES: In the case of small business, a university career is of more doubtful advantage. If a man is to run the whole thing himself, he must begin when he is young and when he is still content with very small earnings... [*A page of typescript is missing at this point*] *...think the discussion has only served to indicate the outlines of this great question and to show how much there is in it. There can be no doubt that in these days businessmen are more in need of learning than any other class, because their responsibilities are, perhaps, greater than those of most people. Equally, I think, the universities have something to learn about business, and to me it is really good to know that the great centres of learning are thinking more and more about their responsibilities to the business world and the development on better lines of this most important of all social services.*

If as a result of to-night's talk nothing more happens than that a million listeners will henceforth connect the two ideas of education and business, the trouble, such as it is, involved will have been amply worthwhile. A million seeds full of promise of good will have been sown, and we may look for even better things from both education and business in coming generations.

May I, as Chairman, in conclusion, on behalf of everyone of the listeners, express our deep sense of obligation both to Mr J. M. Keynes and Mr Ernest Walls for all that they have told us from their respective and equally authoritative points of view.

On Reading Books

[1 June 1936][1]

An edited version of this broadcast appeared in *The Listener* for 10 June 1936. Below is Keynes's original text. The square brackets in the text indicate the material that was edited out of the originally published version.

The first step towards reading – I think you will agree – is to be able to read. Now, according to the law, we are all of us taught to read. Police magistrates are much shocked if a witness cannot read. Yet, in truth, there are very many people, even amongst the highly educated and professional classes, who read with difficulty. I mean by this that they read slowly and with effort, that it tires them – that they do not read as easily as they breathe. On the other hand, I expect that there are many of you, who earn

---

[1] *The Listener,* 10 June 1936, 1126 (edited version); XXVII, 329–35.

your daily bread in ways for which reading is not important and yet do possess one of the best of all gifts – the eye which can pick up the print effortlessly. At any rate to acquire this – and many of you could acquire it merely by practice – is the first step. I emphasise this, because many people think they can read, but they can't. They do not know how far they fall behind the practised reader. We are inclined to think that of six people living in one house all will be much alike in their ability to read. But it is not so. Compare yourself with your friends and neighbours, and find out, first of all, whether you really know how to read – whether, as I have said, you read as easily as you breathe. [Newspapers are good practice in learning how to skip; and, if he is not to lose his time, every serious reader must have this art.]

When you can both walk and skip through a book, what next? I am afraid that I can give you very little advice on contemporary novels. I do not much care for them when I am lazy and relaxed; nor yet when I am contemplative and serious. They do not instruct or comfort or uplift me. It is thought almost a virtue in a modern writer to empty on us the slops of his mind just as they come. And their works are not even trash. For trash can be delightful, and, indeed, a necessary part of one's daily diet.

I read the newspapers because they're mostly trash. But when I glance into this contemporary stuff, I find such heavy-going [such undigested, unenhanced, unintrinsic, unintuitive, such misunderstood, mishandled, misshapen, such muddled handling of human hopes and life; and] without support from the convention and the tradition which in a great age of self-expression can make even the second-rate delightful. So if you want a serious novel, read the old ones – older, at any rate, than the past ten years. [This year's novels are not so good, nor such pleasant easy reading, as Jane Austen's *Emma* or Thomas Hardy's *Tess of the D'Urbervilles* or E. M. Forster's *A Room with a View*. It is only commonsense advice to try these and their fellows first.]

Nevertheless – to begin on the groundfloor – there is one class of author, unpretending, workmanlike, ingenious, abundant, delightful heaven-sent entertainers, in which our age has greatly excelled. There are several of them and we are each entitled to our favourites. I mean Edgar Wallace, Agatha Christie, P. G. Wodehouse – to name mine. I need not mention particular examples, you all know them, and each of them has what is a merit in a favourite author, that their different books are all exactly the same. There is a great purity in these writers, a remarkable absence of falsity and fudge, so that they live and move, serene, Olympian and aloof, free from any pretended contact with the realities of life, each in his world of phantasy moving through the heavens according to its own laws. There is no more perfect relaxation than these.

It is the mark of a species of work in which a particular period excels that even the inferior examples of it have some merit. On this test memoirs and biographies are our best speciality today. [Perhaps we owe it partly to Lytton Strachey that certain repressions and reserves which had a stranglehold on the last generation have sufficiently relaxed to let a little truth and character and the colour of life peep through. Virginia Woolf, who reads *all* of them, tells me that at least nine out of ten can be enjoyed.] The memoir or skimming autobiography is something which our generation *en masse* has somehow learned to write. The very old-fashioned are still too anecdotal and regard their autobiographies as no more than a last opportunity to tell once again all the good stories they have told before. But today a great many of such writers achieve much more than this. I could mention a number. Laura Knight's *Grease Paint and Oil Paint* and Eleanor Farjeon's *A Nursery in the Nineties,* both out this spring, are excellent examples. Or to go back three or four years, Karsavina's *Theatre Street* is a sweet book. Many even of the lives of public characters, who were distinguished in the War – books which were unreadable written in the earlier fashion – have much interest and charm. I particularly enjoyed one which did not attract much notice, the Life of Lord Wester Wemyss by his wife.[2] But [as Virginia Woolf says] this is a class in which it is safe today to choose almost at random; so much more agreeable and amusing, so much more touching, bringing so much more of the pattern of life, than the daydreams of a housemaid, or, alternatively, the daydreams of a nervous wreck,

---

[2] Lady Wemyss, *Life and Letters of the First Lord Wemyss.*

which is the average modern novel. And in this context it is not out of place to mention Winston Churchill's enthralling history, so largely a memoir, of the World War.[3] Even two out of the few recent novels I have read and enjoyed, J. R. Ackerley's *Hindoo Holiday* and David Garnett's *Beany Eye* are, in fact, fragments of memoirs. It is a mixed lot you see. But they have splinters of truth and life in them. Besides we are just ready to be taken back, as a fair sprinkling of these books do take us, to the high comedy, the charm and security, of the Edwardian age in which most of us grew up. The early Victorian humours have grown a little stale by now, a little artificial, stereotyped and overdone. But the Edwardian age is near enough for us quickly to recognise hints and to know truth from falsehood. We want only to be reminded what it was like, and the research of times past in our own memories will do the rest. Our nostalgia is for the charmed years before the War. [We need only a few hints of how we lived then, a few old photographs to bring back the taste of the biscuits we ate and the inner feeling in the whole body of what it was like to be alive in the reign of King Edward and Queen Alexandra.]

[The explanation of the comparative excellence of this class of writing is to be found, perhaps, in the principle that, if we cannot have art which is rare and particularly rare today, the next best is truth and actual experience. There is not much art in any writing today. But in the memoirs and autobiographies

---

[3] *The World Crisis.*

we seem to have caught the knack of recording quite a fair modicum of truth. And when this can be achieved, the memoirs of any age are delightful. I picked up the other day in a catalogue of remainders (the book was published in 1931, but failed, I suppose, to catch the public) the first English translation of *The Book of My Life* by Jerome Cardan, the Italian physician, philosopher and mathematician who lived in the sixteenth century, one of the earliest known of frank confessions and revealing autobiography, and a remarkable example of it.]

There is not much contemporary poetry to recommend. But we have one poet, the Anglo-American, T. S. Eliot, whose name will be spread, I believe, ever more widely as our ears become attuned to him. Two books of his have lately come our way, *Murder in the Cathedral,* not a thriller as the title teasingly suggests, but a religious drama in verse concerning the murder of Thomas à Becket, and his *Collected Poems 1909–1935* [which between them, Mr Eliot tells us, contain all of his poetry which he wishes to preserve]. Here we have, I am sure, the outstanding poetry of our generation, poetry in the great tradition with music and meaning. Mr Eliot's underlying significance and allusion is often obscure; but he has the rarest of possessions, the ear of a poet, and the music of his speech is apparent as soon as the reader becomes a little familiar with it, and the craft with which he freshly echoes older poetry, and the associations of word and meaning.

What seas what shores what grey rocks and
   what islands
What water lapping the bow
And scent of pine and the woodthrush sing-
   ing through the firs
What images return
O my daugher.

There are many branches of knowledge today
which are in no condition to be successfully and de-
cently popularised. Much of anthropology and the
history of very early civilisation is, however, in the
stage where strange facts are being collected; [and
even when some of the facts are disputed by
other experts, it is intelligible reading for any of
us; for example, *Adam's Ancestors* by Leakey, The *Old
Stone Age* by Miles Burkitt and Dr Woolley's account
of Sumeria. I advise the common reader to sample
the current output of these fascinating subjects to
see if they suit his taste.] But philosophy and phys-
ics, for example, are certainly no food for him just
now and most popular books about them are better
avoided. They flatter to deceive. I am not quite sure
in which class that exciting, dangerous subject, psy-
chology, now falls. But, for the moment, I am afraid,
my own subject of political economy is scarcely fit
for the general public; though a popular exposition
may again be possible when the experts have become
clearer amongst themselves. One book there is, however, falling within this field which every serious
citizen will do well to look into – the extensive

description of *Soviet Communism* by Mr and Mrs Sidney Webb. It is on much too large a scale, to be called a popular book, but the reader should have no difficulty in comprehending the picture it conveys. Until recently events in Russia were moving too fast and the gap between paper professions and actual achievements was too wide for a proper account to be possible . But the new system is now sufficiently crystallised to be reviewed. The result is impressive. The Russian innovators have passed, not only from the revolutionary stage but also from the doctrinaire stage.

There is little or nothing left which bears any special relation to Marx and Marxism as distinguished from other systems of socialism. They are engaged in the vast administrative task of making a completely new set of social and economic institutions work smoothly and successfully over a territory so extensive that it covers one-sixth of the land surface of the world. Methods are still changing rapidly in response to experience. The largest scale empiricism and experimentalism which has ever been attempted by disinterested administrators is in operation. Meanwhile the Webbs have enabled us to see the direction in which things appear to be moving and how far they have got. It is an enthralling work, because it contains a mass of extraordinarily important and interesting information concerning the evolution of the contemporary world. It leaves me with a strong desire and hope that we in this country may discover how to combine an unlimited readiness to experiment with changes in political and economic methods and institutions, whilst preserving traditionalism and a sort of careful conservatism, thrifty of everything which has human experience behind it, in every branch of feeling and of action.

[May I conclude with a little general advice from one who can claim to be an experienced reader to those who have learnt to read but have not yet gained experience? A reader should acquire a wide general acquaintance with books *as such,* so to speak. He should approach them with all his senses; he should know their touch and their smell. He should learn how to take them in his hands, rustle their pages and reach in a few seconds a first intuitive impression of what they contain. He should, in the course of time, have touched many thousands, at least ten times as many as he really reads. He should cast an eye over books as a shepherd over sheep, and judge them with the rapid, searching glance with which a cattle-dealer eyes cattle. He should live with more books than he reads, with a penumbra of unread pages, of which he knows the general character and content, fluttering round him. This is the purpose of libraries, one's own and other people's, private and public. It is also the purpose of good bookshops, both new and second hand, of which there are still some, and would that there were more. A bookshop is not like a railway booking-office which one approaches knowing that one wants. One should enter it vaguely, almost in a dream, and allow what is there freely to attract and influence the eye. To walk the rounds of the bookshops, dipping in as curiosity dictates, should be an afternoon's entertainment. Feel no shyness or compunction in taking it. Bookshops exist to provide it; and the booksellers welcome it, well knowing how it will end. It is a habit to acquire in boyhood.]

The Arts Council: Its Policy and Hopes

[8 July 1945][1]

By 1939 Keynes had a record of extensive involvement in the arts. He had amassed a substantial collection of paintings. He was a founder and substantial supporter of the London Artists' Association, an income-support scheme for selected artists. He had been treasurer of the Camargo Ballet Society which was the only organisation in London for the production of ballet between the death of Diaghilev and the founding of the Vic-Wells Ballet (now the Royal Ballet). In 1933–6 he was involved in founding and building the Arts Theatre in Cambridge which opened on the evening before the publication of the *General Theory*. He had largely financed the theatre himself. He nursed it into financial health and, in 1938, transformed the Arts Theatre Limited into a trust as a memorial to his parents' service to the town

---

[1] *The Listener,* 12 July 1945, 31–2; XXVIII, 367–72.

and the University over the previous half century. By 1936, his connections were sufficiently well known that he was not an implausible person to lead off a never-broadcast series of articles in *The Listener* on the subject of 'Art and the State' (XXXVIII, 341–9).

With the war he became even more of a national figure in the arts. In November 1941 he became a Trustee of the National Gallery. A month later he was offered the chair of the Committee for the Encouragement of the Arts, known to contemporaries by its initials CEMA. CEMA had been founded in January 1940 to preserve standards in music, drama and the visual arts, to provide access to the arts for people cut off from them by wartime conditions, to encourage popular participation in music and drama, and, through these activities, to assist artists who might otherwise be unemployed by the war. When he offered Keynes the chair, R. A. Butler, the Minister of Education, remarked that 'while the Council's work will still remain emergency war work, it does, I think, point the way to something that might occupy a more permanent place in our social organisation.'[2] Keynes's appointment took effect from 1 April 1942. In the summer of 1944, he became the chair of the organising committee attempting to make Covent Garden the permanent home for national opera and ballet companies and later the chair of the Trustees of the Royal Opera House. From the late summer of

---

[2] KCKP, PP/84/1, R. A. Butler to JMK, 17 December 1941.

1944 he nursed his proposals for the transform-
ation of CEMA into a permanent peace-time Arts
Council of Great Britain, the first such body in the
world. On 8 July 1945, Sir John Anderson, the
Chancellor of the Exchequer, announced that
CEMA would be so incorporated (a process that in
the end would take until July 1946) and that Keynes
would be the first chair. After the Chancellor's
announcement Keynes held a press conference and
spoke on the BBC.

In the early days of the war, when all sources of
comfort to our spirits were at a low ebb, there came
into existence, with the aid of the Pilgrim Trust, a
body officially styled the 'Council for the
Encouragement of Music and the Arts', but commonly known from its initial letters as CEMA It was
the task of CEMA to carry music, drama and pic-
tures to places which otherwise would be cut off
from all contact with the masterpieces of happier
days and times: to air-raid shelters, to war-time hostels, to factories, to mining villages. ENSA was
charged with the entertainment of the Services; the
British Council kept contact with other countries
overseas; the duty of CEMA was to maintain the opportunities of artistic performance for the hard-
pressed and often exiled civilians.

With experience our ambitions and our scope
increased. I should explain that whilst CEMA was

started by private aid, the time soon came when it was sponsored by the Board of Education and entirely supported by a Treasury grant. We were never given much money, but by care and good housekeeping we made it go a long way. At the start our aim was to replace what war had taken away; but we soon found that we were providing what had never existed even in peace time. That is why one of the last acts of the Coalition Government was to decide that CEMA with a new name and wider opportunities should be continued into time of peace. Henceforward we are to be a permanent body, independent in constitution, free from red tape, but financed by the Treasury and ultimately responsible to Parliament, which will have to be satisfied with what we are doing when from time to time it votes us money. If we behave foolishly, any Member of Parliament will be able to question the Chancellor of the Exchequer and ask why. Our name is to be the Arts Council of Great Britain. I hope you will call us the Arts Council for short, and not try to turn our initials into a false, invented word. We have carefully selected initials which we hope are unpronounceable.

I do not believe it is yet realised what an important thing has happened. Strange patronage of the arts has crept in. It has happened in a very English, informal, unostentatious way – half-baked if you like. A semi-independent body is provided with modest funds to stimulate, comfort and support any societies or bodies brought together on private or local initiative which are striving with serious purpose and a reasonable prospect of success to present for public enjoyment the arts of drama, music and painting.

At last the public exchequer has recognised the support and encouragement of the civilising arts of life as part of their duty. But we do not intend to socialise this side of social endeavour. Whatever views may be held by the lately warring parties, whom you have been hearing every evening at this hour, about socialising industry, everyone, I fancy, recognises that the work of the artist in all its aspects is, of its nature, individual and free, undisciplined, unregimented, uncontrolled. The artist walks where the breath of the spirit blows him. He cannot be told his direction; he does not know it himself. But he leads the rest of us into fresh pastures and teaches us to love and to enjoy what we often begin by rejecting, enlarging our sensibility and purifying our instincts. The task of an official body is not to teach or to censor, but to give courage, confidence and opportunity. Artists depend on the world they live in and the spirit of the age. There is no reason to suppose that less native genius is born into the world in the ages empty of achievement than in those brief periods when nearly all we most value has been brought to birth. New work will spring up more abundantly in unexpected quarters and in unforeseen shapes when there is a universal opportunity for contact with traditional and contemporary arts in their noblest forms.

But do not think of the Arts Council as a school-
master. Your enjoyment will be our first aim. We
have but little money to spill, and it will be you
yourselves who will by your patronage decide in the
long run what you get. In so far as we instruct, it is
a new game we are teaching you to play – and to
watch. Our wartime experience has led us already to
one clear discovery: the unsatisfied demand and the
enormous public for serious and fine entertainment.
This certainly did not exist a few years ago. I do not
believe that it is merely a war-time phenomenon. I
fancy that the BBC has played a big part, the pre-
dominent part, in creating this public demand, by
bringing to everybody in the country the possibility
of learning these new games which only the few
used to play, and by forming new tastes and habits
and thus enlarging the desires of the listener and his
capacity for enjoyment. I am told that today when a
good symphony concert is broadcast as many as five
million people may listen to it. Their ears become
trained. With what anticipation many of them look
forward if a chance comes their way to hear a live
orchestra and to experience the enhanced excitement and concentration of attention and emotion,
which flows from being one of a great audience all
moved together by the surge and glory of an orchestra in being, beating in on the sensibilities of
every organ of the body and of the apprehension.
The result is that half the world is being taught to
approach with a livelier appetite the living performer
and the work of the artist as it comes from his own

hand and body, with the added subtlety of actual flesh and blood.

I believe that the work of the BBC and the Arts Council can react backwards and forwards on one another to the great advantage of both. It is the purpose of the Arts Council to feed these newly aroused and widely diffused desires. But for success we shall have to solve what will be our biggest problem, the shortage – in most parts of Britain the complete absence – of adequate and suitable buildings. There never were many theatres in this country or any concert-halls or galleries worth counting. Of the few we once had, first the cinema took a heavy toll and then the blitz; and anyway the really suitable building for a largish audience which the modern engineer can construct had never been there. The greater number even of large towns, let alone the smaller centres, are absolutely bare of the necessary bricks and mortar. And our national situation today is very unfavourable for a quick solution. Houses for householders have to come first.

And so they should. Yet I plead for a certain moderation from our controllers and a few crumbs of mortar. The re-building of the community and of our common life must proceed in due proportion between one thing and another. We must not limit our provision too exclusively to shelter and comfort to cover us when we are asleep and allow us no convenient place of congregation and enjoyment when we are awake. I hope that a reasonable allotment of resources will be set aside each year for the repair and erection of the buildings we shall need. I hear that in Russia theatres and concert-halls are given a very high priority for building.

And let such buildings be widely spread throughout the country. We of the Arts Council are greatly concerned to decentralise and disperse the dramatic and musical and artistic life of the country, to build up provincial centres and to promote corporate life in these matters in every town and country. It is not our intention to act on our own where we can avoid it. We want to collaborate with local authorities and to encourage local institutions and societies and local enterprise to take the lead. We already have regional offices in Birmingham, Cambridge, Manchester, Nottingham, Bristol, Leeds, Newcastle-on-Tyne, Cardiff and Edinburgh. For Scotland and for Wales special committees have been established. In Glasgow, in particular, the work of the Citizens Theatre is a perfect model of what we should like to see established everywhere, with their own playwrights, their own company and an ever-growing and more appreciative local public. We have great hopes of our new Welsh Committee and of the stimulus it will give to the special genius of the Welsh people. Certainly in every blitzed town in this country one hopes that the local authority will make provision for a central group of buildings for drama and music and art. There could be no better memorial of a war to save the freedom of the spirit of the individual. We look forward to the time when the theatre and the concert-hall and the gallery will be a living element in everyone's upbringing, and regular attendance at the theatre and at concerts a part of organised education. The return of the BBC to regional programmes may play a great part in reawakening local life and interest in all these matters. How satisfactory it would be if different parts of this country would again walk their several ways as they once did and learn to develop something different from their neighbours and characteristic of themselves. Nothing can be more damaging than the excessive prestige of metropolitan standards and fashions. Let every part of Merry England be merry in its own way. Death to Hollywood.

But it is also our business to make London a great artistic metropolis, a place to vist and to wonder at. For this purpose London today is half in ruin. With the loss of the Queen's Hall there is no proper place for concerts. The Royal Opera House at Covent Garden has been diverted to other purposes throughout the war. The Crystal Palace has been burnt to the ground. We hope that Covent Garden will be re-opened early next year as the home of opera and ballet. The London County Council has already allotted a site for a National Theatre. The Arts Council has joined with the Trustees of the Crystal Palace in the preparation of plans to make that once again a great People's Palace.

No one can yet say where the tides of the times will carry our new-found ship. The purpose of the

the Arts Council of Great Britain is to create an environment to breed a spirit, to cultivate an opinion,
to offer a stimulus to such purpose that the artist
and the public can each sustain and live on the other
in that union which has occasionally existed in the
past at the great ages of a communal civilised life.

V
World War II

Six broadcasts between May 1939 and July 1944 make up this section. They relate to the final stages of pre-war rearmament, to Keynes's proposals for wartime finance published as *How to Pay for the War* on 27 February 1940, and to Keynes period as a Treasury adviser on both wartime and post-war issues that came with his appointment as a member of the Chancellor of the Exchequer's Consultative Council on 1 July 1940 and his being given an office in the building on 12 August.

Will Re-armament Cure Unemployment?

[23 May 1939][1]

This broadcast took place against a backcloth of an announcement on 15 February of a 40 per cent rise in defence expenditures in Britain for the fiscal year 1939–40, the German occupation of Prague on 15 March 1939 which made a nonsense of Hitler's promise at Munich to respect the undefended new Czech frontier, the Anglo-French guarantee of Poland's territorial integrity of 30 March, the announcement of the introduction of conscription in Britain on 26 April and the beginnings of staff conversations with the French early in May.

We have suffered so long from severe unemployment that we have come to regard this state of affairs as a chronic malady. Those in authority have refused

---

[1] *The Listener*, 1 June 1939. 1142–3; XXI, 528–32.

to believe that it could be cured by large-scale state expenditure on housing and other needed improvements. If this were correct, it would follow that neither can it be cured by large-scale state expenditure on armaments, of all forms of expenditure the most unproductive. But, for reasons beyond our control, the grand experiment is to be made. In rearming this country, shall we, by accident so to speak, cure unemployment? This is a most exciting question for the workers – and also, I may add, for the economists. What are the arguments? They are not very simple. But they are not very difficult either. So I will try to explain them.

The Government is likely to spend this year under all heads upwards of £250 million above what it spent last year. Obviously more men will be employed making what the Government buys. How far will this be offset by fewer men being employed in other directions? For instance, the taxpayer will pay more and spend less, which means that fewer men will be employed making what the taxpayer would otherwise buy. But the Chancellor of the Exchequer has decided this year that there is to be only a modest increase in taxes. So the deduction to be made on this head is not large. Again, private investment of the ordinary peacetime character may fall off, on new housing for example, either because of a very natural lack of confidence in the prospects, or because it is difficult to get the necessary finance, or because the Government has taken away for its own purposes the specialised labour which alone is able to tackle the job. Moreover, some of the Government expenditure will be spent on imports or will employ labour which would otherwise provide exports. It is difficult to say beforehand how large these offsets will be. Up to date it is not clear that total private investment is falling away very much, though its character may be changing. Private firms and local authorities will be spending a lot of money on ARP beyond what is included in the Government's Budget. Firms with large Government orders are having to extend their permanent plant. A substantial increase in private shipbuilding is in prospect, as a result of Government subsidies. And this is scarcely the time for economising in transport improvements, when smooth and rapid movements of people and of goods may be all important. On the other hand, it is inevitable that there is a good deal of private work which will be postponed for less anxious times. My own guess is that the net decline in other investment will only be large if the Government, on purpose or because they can't help it, put difficulties in the way of people getting hold of finance or of labour. And there will be no occasion to put such difficulties in the way, until we are approaching the full employment of the labour which is both of the required kind and in the right place.

This brings us up to the kernel of our problem and to the question about which there is the most difference of opinion between experts. How many of the men now unemployed are capable of being employed on the particular jobs offering? Even the optimists would not put the proportion higher than two-fifths or perhaps three-fifths of the men now registered as unemployed. And I, who am reckoned an optimist in this matter, agreed that even the lower of these proportions can only be reached as the result of very good organisation by the Government and by industry and of very good will on the part of the trade unions. I know that too often action is not taken until six months or a year too late and then only in response to great pressure from public opinion – a poor substitute for the foresight of true statesmanship; but I expect that the Government will act in the end – they generally do. If any trade unionists and heads of private business who are listening to me show themselves quicker in the uptake than the Government, that will do no harm. For the work can only be done if men are drafted into jobs to which they are not accustomed, and sometimes away from home, and if the skilled men are willing to work in with unskilled men who have to be taught a good deal. Trade unionists have many things of which they can properly complain. But I hope that at this time and in this matter they will be easy and reasonable, for the sake of all of us; and for the sake of themselves, too, because it is only by this means that we can use this opportunity to make a big impression on the curse of continuing unemployment.

The Economist newspaper has given some examples of how acute the problem is likely to be in particular cases. They calculate that if all the unemployed recorded in the aircraft and motor-car industry were to be put to work, they could only supply about a quarter of the Government's increased demand. But perhaps this does not allow nearly enough for the increasing efficiency of production and for overtime by those already in work. If all those concerned behave in a practical way, I see no reason to think that the Government programme cannot be carried through – and without undue interference with other work.

My final guess is that the total national expenditure at home on general investment, public and private, and on armaments not provided out of taxes, may be as much as £200 million more than it was last year. Let us call it £150 million to be on the safe side. How many men will this employ? Somewhere about 600,000, if all the work were to be done by men now unemployed. But this would be a large exaggeration. Men already employed will put in more work and bring home more wages. Perhaps half the extra work may get done this way. If so, the direct effect of the armament expenditure may be to take 300,000 men off the dole. I fancy that even the pessimists would reckon that a fairly conservative figure.

That is the first part of the story. But it is only the first part. As a result of spending £150 million extra, all sorts of people will have bigger incomes. Not all of it will be extra, for those who used to be unemployed will no longer have the dole. But a good proportion will be extra; and those who get it, being ordinary sort of people, will spend most of it. This expenditure of theirs will employ another lot of people, and so on. The money, in the old phrase, will circulate. By how much will this second effect multiply the first effect? It is not easy to say. We have only lately begun to look at the problem just this way, and the statisticians have not yet collected enough material for a safe forecast. I must leave out the details and give you my own estimate for what it is worth, and I will try to be on the safe side. In places where I was more easily open to contradiction than I am on the air, I have given bigger figures all through than I am giving you here. But the figures I am giving are sufficient to establish the argument. Let us put the multiplier effect, as it is called, of the subsequent waves of expenditure, at two-thirds of the initial impulse. Two-thirds of the 300,000 men primarily employed is 200,000, which means that 500,000 men will be taken off the dole altogether. Now this secondary expenditure will be much better spread and easier to meet than the initial expenditure. For the extra wages and incomes will be spent in shops all over the country on all sorts of things. It will not be concentrated on a few special industries.

We reach the conclusion, therefore, that, as compared with last year, the number of the unemployed should fall in the course of the year by 500,000 as a minimum. And some people think that a good case can be made out for putting the estimate half as big again as this, or even double. And this isn't the end. Two hundred thousand young men are going to be called up; and the raising of the school-leaving age this autumn will make a big cut in the numbers of lads coming forward.

What a difference all this makes! It is not an exaggeration to say that the end of abnormal unemployment is in sight. And it isn't only the unemployed who will feel the difference. A great number besides will be taking home better money each week. And with the demand for efficient labour outrunning the supply, how much more comfortable and secure everyone will feel in his job. There will be other reasons for plenty of anxiety. But one of the worst anxieties is anxiety about getting and keeping work. There should be less of that than for years past.

I have a special extra reason for hoping that trade unionists will do what they can to make this big transition to fuller employment work smoothly. I began by saying that the grand experiment has begun. If it works, if expenditure on armaments really does cure unemployment, I predict that we shall never go back all the way to the old state of affairs. If we can cure unemployment for the wasted purposes of armaments, we can cure it for the productive purposes of peace. Good may come out of evil. We may learn a trick or two which will come in useful when the day of peace comes, as in the fullness of time it must.

Should Saving be Compulsory?

[11 March 1940][1]

Keynes's conversation with Donald Tyerman, deputy editor of *The Economist*, followed hard on the publication of *How to Pay for the War*, itself a landmark in his public campaign to finance the war in a non-inflationary manner through increased taxation and compulsory savings that had started with his articles 'Paying for the War' in *The Times* on 14 and 15 December 1939.

> TYERMAN: *How are we going to pay for the war? That is what we all want to know. It isn't just a matter of money. It is a matter of men and materials. We really pay for the war by producing more things for the Government and consuming less ourselves. We have got to work harder than in peace time. We have got to turn out more goods. That is the first step. And at the same time we have got to use less and spend less than we do in peace time. It is not easy. If we work harder, that is, longer hours with more people at work, women and so on,*

---

[1] *The Listener*, 508–9; XXII, 111–17.

then between us we earn more *than we did before the war – and if we are not careful we shall spend* more *instead of* less. *This is where Mr Keynes's plan comes in. He wants to postpone part of our pay so that we can't spend it now. Then, when the war is over, we can have it all back. That is what you are trying to do, Mr Keynes, isn't it, stop us from spending so much now?*

KEYNES: Yes. It is obvious that we must work harder – more men and women in employment and longer overtime. This means that more money will be earned; and by the time we have improved our organisation for war output in the way we must (we are a long way off that yet), the extra money taken home at the end of the week will be very substantial indeed. Bigger output and bigger earnings are just what we want. But they will create a serious problem all the same. The money will have been earned in making stuff for the Government, not in making more for the public to purchase. So it will not increase the amount of goods in the shops available for the public to buy. What follows? More money to spend and less stuff in the shops. There can be only one result if the money is spent. Prices must go up until the goods are so dear that it takes all the increased earnings to buy them. That is what happened in the last war. But what a silly business it was. It meant that those of us who had increased earnings were simply wasting them. And those who had no more money than before were badly hit because at these higher prices their earnings bought so much less.

Yet there is a way out of all this nonsense. During the war the resources do not exist to provide more goods for consumption. But after the war the opposite will be true. We shall be able to produce more than we can easily market. So I propose that everyone should put off spending a proportion of his earnings until that time comes.

TYERMAN: *So your argument is that you have got to force people to save that bit extra. I know a lot of people don't like your scheme because they think it is really an attack on wages. One working man has written me a letter saying: 'Your idea of grabbing some of our small wages compulsorily is a form of Hitlerism.' He goes on to say that the money could be got from more taxes on people who are well off.*

KEYNES: Your friend has a pretty foggy idea of Hitlerism. In Germany the wages are fixed at the lowest possible level and there is very little to buy with them, and there is no proposal to give anything back afterwards. But if he means that we cannot fight Hitlerism, which takes such enormous sacrifices from Germany, without making some sacrifice ourselves, he is quite right. It is not my proposal which will cause the sacrifice. That will be inevitable under any proposal. My object is to divide the sacrifice fairly. And that brings me to his suggestion that the rich can pay for this war. To a large extent they can and should. My plan puts on them by far the greater share of the burden. But the notion that in a war like this the working classes can increase their earnings and then actually take advantage of this to consume more now is surely somewhat unreasonable. Sir John Simon has shown that if you took away the whole of the income of those with £10,000 a year or more, it would only pay for the war for a few days in the year. If you take away the whole of everyone's income in excess of £10 a week, you would only meet about two-thirds of the cost. So it is necessary that those with less than £10 a week must take a share.

TYERMAN: *I can see that. It's a plain matter of fact. But why couldn't you get the same result by voluntary methods, just by simply asking people to save that much more? Won't your scheme damage our fine voluntary effort? I have already heard people saying: 'If I'm going to be forced to save, why should I save of my own accord?'*

KEYNES: I hope everyone will buy all the savings certificates he can and will join one of Sir Robert Kindersley's savings groups. Sir Robert Kindersley and his organisation are doing splendid work. I would not willingly say a word to hinder them. They are working in an extremely practical way to do just what is wanted. Whatever other schemes may be adopted we shall need their efforts and enthusiasm.

And if we were not going to spend more than we spent in the early months of the war, the savings movement might be enough. But this is only a beginning. When the Government is spending half the national income and needs to borrow a hundred million pounds a month, as it soon will be, in addition to the heaviest taxation ever known, and to go on doing this month after month for an indefinite period, we should be deceiving ourselves if we were to believe that we could get on without some further drastic remedy. The voluntary method is vastly preferable. The response is magnificent. If we did not need so much it would provide enough. But to depend on it exclusively when the Government needs half the national income is like trying to raise an army of five million without conscription.

TYERMAN: *Well, what exactly is the way out you want us to take?*

KEYNES: What we need is something like a rule of the road. Remember what the problem is. Consumption will be cut down, anyhow. The stuff will not be there to be consumed. If we try to spend too much of our earnings, all that can happen will be that we shall get in one another's way in spending our money. So let us have a general rule of the road not to get in one another's way. That is what my proposal comes to. All except those who have no margin in their standard of life will be asked to defer spending a part of their earnings which will be put to their credit as their own money to be spent after the war. The trouble is that individual circumstances differ so much. Some people's incomes will have gone up and some will have gone down. Some already have a margin. Others, because their wages are low or because they have young families, have no margin at all. So my proposal needs many safeguards.

TYERMAN: *That seems to me a vastly important point. There are some people who can't really do without anything, people with low earnings or big families as you say. How are you going to look after them?*

KEYNES: To begin with, payments must be steeply graded. I cannot give you all the details here. You will find them in my pamphlet *How to Pay for the War*. A married man with 45s a week or less will have nothing deferred. At 50s, 1s 9d will be deferred. That is to say, temporarily withheld until after the war. At 55s, 3s 6d will be deferred; at 75s, 10s 6d, and so on. A man with £20 a week has eight times the income of a man with 50s. But the income tax he will pay and his income deferment added together will come not to eight times the 50s a week man, but *eighty* times. That is to say, he will pay ten times higher in proportion to his income. If we solve the problem of letting prices rise, as we did in the last war, instead of the £20 a week man paying a much bigger share, it will be the 50s a week man who will be the harder hit in proportion to his income. With my scheme, moreover, it would be possible for the Government to keep down the prices of what has been called an iron ration of the chief necessaries of life.

TYERMAN: *Another of my correspondents writes: 'We say rude things about saving and sacrifice – our life is one long sacrifice. Ask Mr Keynes to keep a family on £3 8s 6d a week and see how much he can save.' What would be the position of a man like that?*

KEYNES: I propose a family allowance of 5s a week in cash for every child under 15. This has nothing to do with the employer or with wages, or indeed with the father. It will be payable to the mother in cash at the Post Office and will be her money. Take your friend with 68s 6d a week, he will have 8s 3d of his pay deferred. But if he has two young children, his wife will receive 10s a week towards their cost. So the family will be actually 1s 9d in pocket and will also have 8s 3d a week accumulating to their credit to spend after the war.

TYERMAN: *You say the deferred pay will be accumulating to their credit. They are not losing it for good. But is this really true? Isn't it frankly a sort of hidden tax?*

KEYNES: That is certainly not the intention. The next lot of safeguards are to make it perfectly clear that the deferred earnings really are the property of the man who earned them. In the case of an insured man they would be collected by stamping a deferred earnings card just like an insurance card. The amount of stamps on the card would show how much stood to the man's credit. He would then have to choose in what institution he wanted to keep his deposit – for example, his friendly society, his trade union or the Post Office Savings Bank.

TYERMAN: *Would it carry interest too?*

KEYNES: Yes. At 2½ per cent. And he would be allowed to apply the money to certain other forms of saving if he preferred – for example, to pay his life insurance premiums, to meet instalments to a building society or to pay off any hire purchase agreements he had made before the war. Generally speaking, he must not spend it on new consumption until after the war. But his friendly society or trade union would be allowed to let him draw on it any time if he was able to show good reason on account of illness or unemployment or special family difficulties. And if he died, it would be released for the use of his dependants. After the war, not quite at once but a little later on when there were again surplus resources, the money would be freely his to do what he liked with.

TYERMAN: *What sort of amount would it come to?*

KEYNES: Take a married man with £5 a week. £41 10s a year will be accumulating to his credit. If the war lasts two-and-a-half-years, he will have over £100 in the bank. And if he has two children his wife will also have collected £65 in cash. Now, isn't this much better than to have the purchasing power permanently taken away from you either by taxes or by high prices? For those are the alternatives.

In the last war, most of the rights to extra expenditure after the war belonged to the richer classes. All the rest of the community owed them a huge sum in the shape of the National Debt. If the Government has to borrow, as it certainly will, someone will have the right to extra expenditure after the war. I want this right to be spread through all classes. The wage-earning class will work harder but they cannot consume more now because it is not there to be consumed. But that is no reason why they should not have the right to extra consumption later on. Under this proposal they would be accumulating several hundred million pounds to their credit in each year.

TYERMAN: *That sounds all very well. But how is it to be paid back after the war?*

KEYNES: There is no more difficulty than in the case of any other part of the National Debt. And you can be quite sure that any government would regard this part of it as the most sacred. But as an extra safeguard, I would like to see a pledge that it will be met after the war by a capital levy or tax on wealth. In many ways there would be something appropriate in this. And it would have another advantage. We could then afford to do something similar for men at the front. It would be extremely unfair if men who have the opportunity of earning wages at home ended up the war with perhaps £100 to their credit under this proposal; whilst those who had been in the Forces ended up with nothing. If we agreed to pay for the scheme by a capital levy, we could afford to credit the men who had been risking their lives with about the same sum which they would have had to their credit if they had stayed at home. Isn't that a great additional attraction and a very fair thing to do?

British Finances after a
Year of War

[13–23 September 1940][1]

In September 1940, with the approval of the
Chancellor of the Exchequer, Sir Kingsley Wood,
Keynes broadcast on the financial problems of
the first year of the war. The broadcast exists in
five versions: Home Service, Empire, American and
Latin American (Spanish and Portuguese). The version published here is the Home Service broadcast
on 23 September and published in *The Listener*.

In general conversation I find people far too
depressed about our finances. The usual opinion
seems to be that the war will leave this country seriously impoverished, and that we are heading
straight for inflation. After looking closely into the

---

[1] *The Listener*, 26 September 1940; 436, 455; XXII, 240–5.

real position, I feel much more buoyant than that. I will tell you my conclusions. And I shall be careful to say only what I am sure I could substantiate.

Take the national wealth. The wastage of national resources, which we have suffered so far, is easily exaggerated. What, as a nation, have we lost in the first year of the war? We have parted with some of our more liquid assets in the shape of gold, etc. mainly to the United States. A million and a half tons of shipping has been sunk by enemy action. Buildings have been destroyed from the air, but only in the last month of the year on an important scale. We have not made good all the current wear and tear of buildings and plant in use. On the other hand, allowing for the big reserves of the main foods and raw materials which the Ministries of Food and Supply have built up, our stocks of commodities, so far from being diminished, are probably increased. After taking all these things into account, our total loss of wealth is certainly not greater than the amount by which we had increased it in the two or three years before the war; which means that after a year of war Great Britain remains richer in national wealth than she was at the beginning of 1937.

Does that surprise you? If so, be of good cheer, and stop thinking that after the war we shall have to lower our standards of life. I see no likelihood of that. On the contrary, I hope that we shall have learnt some things about the conduct of currency and foreign trade, about central controls, and about the capacity of the country to produce which will prevent us from ever relapsing into our pre-war economic morass. There is no reason why most people should not look forward to higher standards of life after the war than they have ever enjoyed yet.

Popular exaggeration is just as great when we come to details. Take ships. Our loss of a million and a half tons of shipping is far from negligible. Yet this loss of ships in the course of a year is no greater than our normal capacity to build new ones in a single year.

In losses by bombing from the air the case is not yet worse. Up to the end of July, before the *blitzkrieg* from the air began, the total damage to property in the previous eleven months could have been made good in a couple of days by the country's peacetime building capacity. In August damage was much more considerable. But even during that month it was certainly far short of what our normal building capacity could have made good within the month. There is not yet an accurate estimate of the heavy destruction in London in the last three weeks. It might be rash of me to say that the damage done since the beginning of August up to date has not been much greater than the normal capacity of our building trade to reinstate within the same period; but I believe that I should not prove far wrong, London is a big place. There can be a mighty power of destruction before the building properties of the country as a whole are seriously touched. A million pounds' worth of destruction is a frightful sight to see. But if we were to suffer a million pounds' worth of damage every night for a year, we should not have lost more than 4 per cent of our buildings and their contents, or more than we could restore in a couple of years. And we have the capacity to replace what is lost by something much better. Some of the major glories of London date from the Great Fire. London will, I should hope, rise from the present mess handsomer and healthier than before.

Fortunately or unfortunately, it is not physically possible to meet more than a small proportion of the costs of war out of our accumulated wealth. We cannot turn council houses into aeroplanes or arterial roads into tanks. The main expense of the war has to be met either by drawing resources from overseas or with what we produce at home here and now. It can be met in no other way. And this has an important moral. Since we must mainly depend, not on our accumulated wealth, but on our daily production, output for war purposes can only be released by our economising in our daily consumption and by our saving all we can from our current incomes. And that brings me to the budget problem. Are we saving and taxing on a scale heavy enough to prevent the social evils of inflation?

We have not adopted the German method of limiting expenditure by strictly rationing a wide range of articles of general consumption. As a method of organising acute scarcity, nothing can be more efficient than this. We admire the skill with which it has been carried out. The elaboration of a system for preventing individuals from doing or getting what they want appears to be a task peculiarly suited to the Prussian genius. Our object in rationing a limited range of articles is a different one, namely, to divert consumption away from certain goods which happen to be for special reasons in short supply. Taking the country as a whole, there has been no significant reduction, apart from voluntary savings, in the scale of peacetime consumption – an average reduction of 5 per cent at the outside. Our problem is a different one, namely, to prevent the better conditions of employment, the overtime earnings and the higher wages, which now prevail, from resulting in a pressure to buy *more* than in peacetime. For we cannot afford that in time of war. If more money is being earned and can be freely spent, a rise of prices can only be prevented if a sufficient proportion of these earnings is recovered by the Government in the shape either of taxes or of saving.

I return, therefore, to my question. Is the Government getting back in taxes and are we saving enough income to prevent an inflationary rise in prices? I shall not be suspected of a tendency to undue optimism in answering this question. I spent all my energies during the early months of the war in calling attention to this danger. I advocated a remedy, namely a system of deferred pay, without the adoption of which I doubted if inflation could be avoided. The Government have not yet adopted this remedy. I am still of the opinion that, sooner or later, some more drastic methods than those yet adopted will be necessary and that no better remedy than my own has been proposed by anyone else. Moreover the opinion is widely spread throughout the financial press that we are already heading for inflation, precisely because the Government have failed to adopt either my remedy or any alternative for it.

Clearly my natural bias would be to agree with this view. Nevertheless I am unable to do so. I am no less convinced than before that new and drastic financial methods will be required when our rate of expenditure is at full flood. But my investigations lead me to the conclusion that there has been no significant degree of budgetary inflation up to date. The British public, rather surprisingly, have underestimated the weight of Sir Kingsley Wood's July Budget. If we calculate on the basis of taxes which are now accruing for subsequent payment, the tax revenue provides for appreciably more than half of that part of our total budget expenditure which we have to finance at home. A considerable further contribution comes from various capital resources. The savings movement has been more successful, in my opinion, than its leaders seem to think. In the early months of the war the published statistics were misleading, since they included a large proportion of money which was not newly saved but merely transferred. Today they include very little which is not new money. At any rate these various sources between them have been very nearly adequate up to date.

After all, the real test of inflation is the actual movement of prices. At the beginning of the war and for some months after there was a considerable rise in the price of imports due to freights, insurance, exchange and a sharp rise of prices abroad. Domestic prices did not rise, and have not risen, by more than half the rise in import prices. Moreover international prices are now falling, whilst the exchange value of sterling is now stable for all purposes. The result is that the domestic price level is not now rising. There is none of the evidence of domestic inflation, which, if it exists, must show itself beyond all concealment, as it showed itself during the last war, in steeply rising prices, shop-shortages, queues and an exhaustion of retailers' stocks. No such symptoms are apparent.

The financial position is, therefore, still under control. All the more reason for keeping it so. Much greater economic sacrifices are in prospect for us. We are so little touched at present because we are only beginning to put forth our economic strength. It has not been necessary in the first year of war to ask of us any serious economic restrictions. This second year is, in truth, the first year of the real war for Britain. We have the freshness of a fighter in the first round of the combat; whereas Germany has already suffered the nervous tension and muscular exhaustion of five years of prodigious effort. But we must not be deceived about what will be required from us when we are fighting and producing up to our full capacity. My point is that in the financial field nothing has happened up to date to give us excessive anxiety. So it is well worthwhile to have a policy, however drastic, about taxes and savings, wages and prices, which will keep the position as sound and good as it is now.

Tax on Lower Incomes

[22 December 1941][1]

In December 1941 Keynes made a brief broadcast on the financial achievements of the past year, in particular the measures introduced in the 1941 Budget – a broadening of the income tax which brought about four million new taxpayers into the income tax net for the first time, and the introduction of post-war credits.

Last Friday, the Chancellor of the Exchequer explained to you the importance of paying readily the income tax which most weekly wage earners will find deducted from their pay beginning next month.

I have a point about this which is both interesting and important. I can make it clear in a few sentences.

---

[1] XXII, 356–7.

The goods which can be supplied to the public are limited in amount. There is not enough manpower to make more for you. There are not enough ships to bring more into the country.

Thus, unless prices go up, the total amount which can be bought in the shops and spent on rent, light, fuel, travelling, entertainment and all else you can spend your money on is a fixed amount. It can't be increased. We can actually calculate it, because we know with some accuracy, both quantities and values. It comes to about £12 millon a day, at the prices you are now paying. But your personal wages and other incomes, before you have paid your income tax, are more like £16 million a day. All these are figures of personal incomes. Mr and Mrs John Citizen and all the other Mr and Mrs Citizens are, between them, getting incomes of £16 million a day. All the things on which you and the others can spend this money are worth only £12 million a day. That means there is a balance of £4 million a day, which it is useless for you to try to spend. For if you do try to spend it, there can only be muddle and waste and nuisance. Either prices are forced up, so that you pay more money for the same things, or the money just cannot be spent, for there is nothing to spend it on. But the effort to spend it, besides raising prices, will mean more black markets, longer queues, more waiting, more disappointment; and no one will be better off except at his neighbour's expense. The best system of rationing we can organise will not prevent all this.

Therefore, I say, there is an excess of £4 million a day which must not be spent. Personal savings are now, I suppose, in the neighbourhood of £2 million a day, not bad, very good comparatively, but it covers only half the gap. So that a balance of another £2 million a day still remains. I'm giving you round figures.

A tax on earnings is much the fairest way to meet this. For such a tax can take proper account of the size of people's incomes, and their family responsibilities, which is not possible with any other kind of tax.

If you agree with me that the money must not be spent, and if you agree with me that people left to themselves will not save the whole amount required – and even if they did, the war has to be paid for – is not a tax on in[come the right policy?

Besides, there is a concession which you must not forget. A large part of what those with small earnings have to pay in income tax is only taken from them temporarily, and they will be given a post-war credit, to be paid back when the war is over. Take the married man who earns £4 a week. If he has a child, he pays nothing. If he has no children, he pays nearly 6s a week in income tax – practically the whole of which will be returned to him after the war. How can he complain! A bachelor pays a bit more, and so he should.

I emphasise the fairness of the system, because for many taxpayers it is new – by next year there will be more than three million income tax payers who have never paid income tax before – because it looks worse than it is, and chiefly because people will pay cheerfully if they can see that it is fair. Besides which, the fact remains that even if the tax were not charged, you could buy no more goods than you are buying now.

How Much Does Finance Matter?

[23 March 1942][1]

By the spring of 1942, Keynes, many of his Treasury colleague and the economists in the Economic Section of the Offices of the War Cabinet were becoming involved in discussions that attempted to shape the post-war world. Domestically there were discussion of social insurance surrounding the preparation of the Beveridge Report and proposals for a post-war employment policy that had emerged from the pen of James Meade of the Economic Section. As a part of a series of BBC talks on 'Post-War Planning' Keynes contributed one on the importance of finance.[2]

---

[1] *The Listener*, 2 April 1942, 437–8; XXVII, 264–70.
[2] Keynes's reference on page 222 to Mr. Osborne's talk was to F. J. Osborne, 'Compensation for Changed Land Values' *The Listener*, 10 March 1942, 365–6.

215

For some weeks at this hour you have enjoyed the day-dreams of planning. But what about the nightmare of finance? I am sure there have been many listeners who have been muttering:

'That's all very well, but how is it to be paid for?'

Let me begin by telling you how I tried to answer an eminent architect who pushed on one side all the grandiose plans to rebuild London with the phrase: 'Where's the money to come from?' 'The money?' I said. 'But surely, Sir John, you don't build houses with money? Do you mean that there won't be enough bricks and mortar and steel and cement?' 'Oh no', he replied, 'of course there will be plenty of all that'. 'Do you mean', I went on, 'that there won't be enough labour? For what will the builders be doing if they are not building houses?' 'Oh no, that's all right', he agreed. 'Then there is only one conclusion. You must be meaning, Sir John, that there won't be enough *architects*'. But there I was trespassing on the boundaries of politeness. So I hurried to add: 'Well, if there are bricks and mortar and steel and concrete and labour and architects, why not assemble all this good material into houses?' But he was, I fear, quite unconvinced. 'What I want to know', he repeated, 'is where the money is coming from'. To answer that would have got him and me into deeper water than I cared for, so I replied rather shabbily: 'The same place it is coming from now.' He might have countered (but he didn't): 'Of course I know that money is not the slightest use whatever.

But, all the same, my dear sir, you will find it a devil of a business not to have any.'

A question of pace and preference

Had I given him a good and convincing answer by saying that we build houses with bricks and mortar, not with money? Or was I only teasing him? It all depends what he really had in mind. He might have meant that the burden of the national debt, the heavy taxation, the fact that the banks have lent so much money to the Government and all that, would make it impossible to borrow money to pay the wages of the makers of the raw material, the building labour and even the architects. Or he might have meant something quite different. He could have pointed out very justly that those who were making houses would have to be supported meanwhile with the means of subsistence. Will the rest of us, after supporting ourselves, have enough margin of output of food and clothing and the like, directly or by foreign trade, to support the builders as well as ourselves whilst they are at work?

In fact was he really talking about money? Or was he talking about resources in general – resources in a wide sense, not merely bricks and cement and architects? If the former, if it was some technical problem of finance that was troubling him, then my answer was good and sufficient. For one thing, he was making the very usual confusion between the problem of finance for an individual and the problem for the community as a whole. Apart from this, no doubt there is a technical problem, a problem which we have sometimes bungled in the past, but one which today we understand much more thoroughly. It would be out of place to try to explain it in a few minutes on the air, just as it would be to explain the technical details of bridge-building or the internal combustion engine or the surgery of the thyroid gland. As a technician in these matters I can only affirm that the technical problem of where the *money* for reconstruction is to come from can be solved, and therefore should be solved.

Perhaps I can go a little further than this. The technical problem at the end of this war is likely to be a great deal easier to handle than it was at the end of the last war when we bungled it badly. There are two chief reasons for this. The Treasury is borrowing money at only half the rate of interest paid in the last war, with the result that the interest paid in 1941 on the new debt incurred in this war was actually more than offset by the relief to national resources of not having a large body of unemployed. We cannot expect that the position will be so good as this at the end of the war. Nevertheless if we *keep* good employment when peace comes (which we can and mean to do), even the post-war Budget problem will not be too difficult. And there is another reason also. In 1919 public opinion and political opinion were determined to get back to 1914 by scrapping at the first possible moment many of the controls which were making the technical task easier. I do not notice today the same enthusiasm to get back to 1939. I hope and believe that this time public opinion will give the technicians a fair chance by letting them retain so long as they think necessary many of the controls over the financial machinery which we are finding useful, and indeed essential, today.

What can we afford to spend?

Now let me turn back to the other interpretation of what my friend may have had at the back of his head – the adequacy of our resources in general, even assuming good employment, to allow us to devote a large body of labour to capital works which would bring in no immediate return. Here is a real problem, fundamental yet essentially simple, which it is important for all of us to try to understand. The first task is to make sure that there is enough demand to provide employment for everyone. The second task is to prevent a demand in excess of the physical possibilities of supply, which is the proper meaning of inflation. For the physical possibilities of supply are very far from unlimited. Our building pro-gramme must be properly proportioned to the resources which are left *after* we have met our daily needs and have produced enough exports to pay for what we require to import from overseas. Immediately after the war the export industries must have the first claim on our attention. I cannot emphasise that too much. Until we have rebuilt our export trade to its former dimensions, we must be prepared for any reasonable sacrifice in the interests of exports. Success in that field is the clue to success all along the line. After meeting our daily needs by production and by export, we shall find ourselves with a certain surplus of resources and of labour available for capital works of improvement. If there is *insufficient* outlet for this surplus, we have unemployment. If, on the other hand, there is an *excess* demand, we have inflation.

To make sure of good employment we must have ready an ample programme of re-stocking and of development over a wide field, industrial, engineering, transport and agricultural – not merely building. Having prepared our blue-prints, covering the whole field of our requirements and not building alone – and these can be as ambitious and glorious as the minds of our engineers and architects and social planners can conceive – those in charge must then concentrate on the vital task of central management, the *pace* at which the programme is put into operation, neither so slow as to cause unemployment nor so rapid as to cause inflation. The proportion of this surplus which can be allocated to building must depend on the order of our preference between different types of project.

With that analysis in our minds, let us come back to the building and constructional plans. It is extremely difficult to predict accurately in advance the scale and pace on which they can be carried out. In the long run almost anything is possible. Therefore do not be afraid of large and bold schemes. Let our plans be big, significant, but not hasty. Rome was not built in a day. The building of the great architectural monuments of the past was carried out slowly, gradually, over many years, and they drew much of their virtue from being the fruit of slow cogitation ripening under the hand and before the eyes of the designer. The problem of pace can be determined rightly only in the light of the competing programmes in all other directions.

The difficulty of predicting accurately the appropriate pace of the execution of the building programme is extremely tiresome to those concerned. You cannot improvise a building industry suddenly or put part of it into cold storage when it is excessive. Tell those concerned that we shall need a building industry of a million operatives directly employed – well and good, it can be arranged. Tell them that we shall need a million-and-a-half or two million – again well and good. But we must let them have in good time some reasonably accurate idea of the target. For if the building industry is to expand in an orderly fashion, it must have some assurance of continuing employment for the larger labour force.

I myself have no adequate data on which to guess. But if you put me against a wall opposite a firing squad, I should, at the last moment, reply that at the present level of prices and wages we might afford in the early post-war years to spend not less than £600 million a year and not more than £800 million on the output of the building industry as a whole. Please remember that this includes repairs and current painting and decorations and replacements as well as all new construction, not merely on houses but also on factories and all other buildings. That, for what it is worth, is my best guess. It covers the activities of private citizens, of firms and companies, of building societies, as well as of local authorities and the central government. Now these are very large sums. Continued, year by year, over a period of ten years or more, they are enormous. We could double in twenty years all the buildings there now are in the whole country. We can do almost anything we like, *given time*. We must not force the pace – that is necessary warning. In good time we can do it all. But we must work to a long-term programme.

Not all planning is expensive. Take the talk of two months ago about planning the countryside. Nothing costly there. To preserve as the national domain for exercise and recreation and the enjoyment and contemplation of nature the cliffs and coastline of the country, the Highlands, the lakes, the moors and fells and mountains, the downs and woodlands furnished with hostels and camping grounds and easy access – that requires no more than the decision to act. For the community as a whole the expense is insignificant. Or take the question of compensation, which Mr Osborn discussed so clearly and so fairly a fortnight ago. Compensation uses up no resources. It is out of one pocket into another and costs nothing to the community as a whole.

Even the planning of London to give space and air and perspective costs nothing to the nation's resources and need not involve a charge on the Budget. There is heaps of room, enough and more than enough, in a re-planned London. We could get all the accommodation we need if a third of the present built-up area was cleared altogether and left cleared. The blitz has uncovered St Paul's to the eyes of this generation. To leave it so will cost nothing to the community as a whole. To build may be costly. Let us offset that expense by a generous policy, here and there, of *not* building.

Where we are using up resources, do not let us submit to the vile doctrine of the nineteenth century that every enterprise must justify itself in pounds, shillings and pence of cash income, with no other denominator of values but this. I should like to see that war memorials of this tragic struggle take the shape of an enrichment of the civic life of every great centre of population. Why should we not set aside, let us say, £50 millions a year for the next twenty years to add in every substantial city of the realm the dignity of an ancient university or a European capital to our local schools and their surroundings, to our local government and its offices, and above all perhaps, to provide a local centre of refreshment and entertainment with an ample theatre, a concert hall, a dance hall, a gallery, a British restaurant, canteens, cafés and so forth. Assuredly we can afford this and much more. Anything we can actually *do* we can afford. Once done, it is *there*.

Nothing can take it from us. We are immeasurably richer than our predecessors. Is it not evident that some sophistry, some fallacy, governs our collective action if we are forced to be so much meaner than they in the embellishments of life?

Yet these must be only the trimmings on the more solid, urgent and necessary outgoings on housing the people, on reconstructing industry and transport and on re-planning the environment of our daily life. Not only shall we come to possess these excellent things with a big programme carried out at a properly regulated pace we can hope to keep employment good for many years to come. We shall, in very fact, have built our New Jerusalem out of the labour which in our former vain folly we were keeping unused and unhappy in enforced idleness.

Bretton Woods

[22 July 1944][1]

From 1–22 July 1944 the representatives of 43 nations met at Bretton Woods, New Hampshire to draft the Articles of Agreement of an International Monetary Fund and an International Bank for Reconstruction and Development. The two institutions had their origins in 1941 plans devised by Keynes and Harry Dexter White of the US Treasury which were refined by intensive, largely Anglo-American discussions during 1943 and early 1944. At the end of the Conference, White, who had chaired the Commission on the Fund, and Keynes, who had chaired that on the Bank, made statements for the evening's BBC news. Both appeared in *The Listener*. Keynes's appears below.

I will not say that the establishment of the Bank for Reconstruction and Development is more important

---

[1] *The Listener*, 27 July 1944, 100; XXVI, 101–3.

than the Monetary Fund but perhaps it is more urgent. UNRRA will provide funds necessary for relief and rehabilitation in the days immediately following liberation but it will not provide finance for more permanent reconstruction and the restoration of industry and agriculture. To fill this gap is one of the main purposes of the Bank which we have been working at in Bretton Woods. Its other main purpose is the development of the less developed areas of the world in the general interests of the standard of life, of conditions of labour, and the expanse of trade everywhere.

The capital which we are aiming at and which we hope eventually to attain is £2,000 million. I can say with confidence that the initial capital of the Bank will not fall short of 2,000 million. This is a vast amount in terms of international lending and should be adequate for all proper requirements for some time to come. The Bank will have some novel principles. In the early days after the war only a few countries and chiefly the United States will have the necessary surplus resources available to invest overseas. How then can the rest of us help and how can the Bank become a genuinely international institution, whilst only the more fortunately placed countries can find large sums for investment during these early days?

The proposal is that it is up to the rest of us to stand behind the credit of the devastated and undeveloped countries and take – each of us – our share in guaranteeing the lenders from ultimate loss.

There are many careful provisions to safeguard the guarantors from excessive loss, but the whole world will join together in a mutual credit insurance pool, as I would describe it, to shoulder risks which private investors might be unwilling to run with future prospects so uncertain and precarious.[2] [As a rule the Bank's loans will not take the form of free cash in the hands of the borrower, which he could use and squander as a free addition to his income, as was so often the case in the past. They will be tied to overseas expenditure – on specific projects, which have been carefully examined and approved. The term specific project will be widely interpreted and any proper scheme for the reconstruction of industry in Liberated Europe or for fresh development will be eligible. The place of expenditure of the loans thus guaranteed will not be tied to the country in which the loans are raised, but will be available for purchases in any part of the world from the manufacturers best able to supply the demand.] I can scarcely exaggerate, the vast benefits which may flow to the world from this great scheme. Resources will be available to reconstruct the liberated areas. Buying power will be available for the output of manufacturers in every country physically capable of meeting the demand. A powerful means will be provided to assist the maintenance of equilibrium in the balance of payments between debtor and

---

[2] The passage in square brackets was deleted by the BBC from the advance script before the broadcast was heard.

creditor countries. There has never been such a far-reaching proposal on so great a scale to provide employment in the present and increase productivity in the future. We have been working quietly away in the cool woods and mountains of New Hampshire and I doubt if the world yet understands how big a thing we are bringing to birth.